MW00608711

FAITH UNDER FIRE
A TRUE STORY OF LOVE, WAR, FAITH AND MIRACLES.

Michael S. Wren

Distributed by:

Granite Publishing and Distribution, L.L.C.
868 North 1430 West • Orem, UT 84057
(801) 229-9023 • Toll Free (800) 574-5779
FAX (801) 229-1924

Printed in the United States of America
by Community Press, Provo, Utah

10 9 8 7 6 5 4 3 2 1

Library of Congress Card Number: 00-105997
ISBN: 1-930980-00-0

In honor of my dear parents.

ACKNOWLEDGMENTS

We wish to express thanks to the following people who have assisted in the production of this story. A very special thank you to our friend Wayne Patterson for his interest and assistance in this work. His time and efforts were invaluable to the successful completion of our story. We also extend deep appreciation to our friend Joylyn Taylor whose comments and proofreading were an essential part of the final publication.

Helaman 5:12 And now my sons, remember, remember, that it is upon the Rock of our Redeemer, who is Christ, the Son of God, that ye must build your foundation; that when the devil shall send forth his mighty winds, yea, his shafts in the whirlwind, yea when all his hail and mighty storm shall beat upon you, it shall have no power over you to drag you down to the gulf of misery and endless woe, because of the Rock upon which ye are built, which is a sure foundation, a foundation whereon if men build, they cannot fall.

FOREWORD

For over thirty years I watched the progression of my father's life. I witnessed an entire range of emotions--from indescribable sorrow to unimaginable joy. I watched him struggle with events that cannot be fully comprehended by those who have not experienced the same things, first-hand. There is not a son who has more respect and love for his father than myself. You are about to read the true story of his life. I wrote the story in the first person so that the reader can more easily *feel* the story, not just read it. The 'Dear Daddy' letters are my own and reflect actual feelings and emotions of those years. In addition, the statements made by mother are added to give perspective and insight to the events as she experienced them.

The biography is intended neither as a political statement about Vietnam nor a comprehensive history of the Special Forces. It is a story of conversion to the Gospel of Jesus Christ in spite of the world and it's troubles, and it is a love story.

Finally, although the story you are about to read is spectacular, and nothing short of miraculous, still this alone does not justify its writing. It is a story of one man's quest to understand, then to incorporate into his life, the principle of *faith*. As you begin reading, it is my hope--and the hope of all our family members--that you will feel the power that faith produces, and the blessings of hope and endurance.

Michael S. Wren

Dear Reader,

My English name is Robert John Wren and my Blackfeet Indian name is Keepippokayo (Many Bears). The following pages contain a true account of the major events of my life. Only at the persistent requests of my eldest son, Mike, have I agreed to share this story. However, in revealing a portion of my wartime experiences, I do not wish to glorify the horrors of war. To the contrary, these occurrences are included only to allow contrast between the dark and light days of my life. There is no glory in rehearsing the cries of bloody, dying friends.

Some years ago a movie was made about a former Green Beret soldier who had been part of a small, handpicked Special Forces team. As one of only a few surviving team members, he came home to America and had trouble adjusting. In this movie, the former Green Beret became angry toward a policeman, and ended up destroying an entire town. This story was a Hollywood myth and is considered an insult to those of us who were actual members of the handpicked team known as *Project Delta*, now known as Delta Force. There were 25 original recon team members, but only a few of us are alive today.

Hollywood depicts a perspiring, bare-chested man with belts of M-60 ammunition crossing his chest. In reality, we wore a soldiers' uniform and never carried M-60 weapons, so we didn't need any belts of ammunition. Hollywood displays a man with a black bandana standing up in front of dozens of enemy machine guns, yet he is never hit by the bullets. In reality, machine gun bullets kill people and black bandanas are not part of a military uniform. Hollywood shows viewers a psychopath shooting up a small town in America. However, neither I, nor my fellow team members, were psychopaths. Hollywood describes a Green Beret team that was trained for difficult missions wherein most of them were killed. Tragically, this is the part of reality they correctly portrayed. Life--and death--were a literal *hell* for those of us who so served, even these many years later.

May you, the reader, see truth as it flows through the following pages. And may you join me in sorrow for the suffering of so many in this world as each of us search to bring peace to our hearts and lives. May you also find hope as you learn of my journey, and hope in the ability a person has to overcome all difficulties and to keep the fires of love burning, even when all seems lost.

Robert J. Wren, Keepippokayo

Chapter One
The Rescue

April, 1949: My mother joined the Mormon Church and had me get dressed in white to get baptized. I was a hard-headed boy from the Blackfeet Indian reservation and I had no spiritual inclinations whatsoever. Though my dear mother tried to teach me of the things of God, my baptism carried no spiritual birth and my confirmation was void of true conversion. Mother said that I could feel peace and happiness in my heart. I wouldn't listen to her. I wish I had.

April, 1966: Enemy machine gun fire was suddenly very intense. Bullets were smashing through our helicopter and pinging around us with an occasional tracer round adding to the terror. An instant later the co-pilot took a direct hit in the chest. Realizing what had happened, the pilot began to pull away to abort our mission, but it was too late. The chopper had been damaged, we lost power and were falling to the ground, right into the enemy which had shot us down. Flying at an altitude of only five hundred feet, we were still miles away from our landing zone when our damaged helicopter began to fall into the dark jungle. Even as we fell, I noticed that the enemy machine guns continued to shoot at us. I figured the enemy was cheering at the sight and were already on their way to where we would soon crash.

I was no stranger to difficult situations, having been shot down three times before. My face and teeth and back had been blasted by grenade shrapnel, I had been gunshot twice, had been surrounded by the dead and dying, and I had seen the faces of men I had been forced to kill. I knew the routine all too well, after the hit of the machine-gun fire I would hope the pilot could provide a controlled descent, then, if we were still alive after the crash landing, I would organize any wounded and panic-filled soldiers for escape and evasion. The H-34 helicopter had a cockpit that was perched several feet higher than the cargo deck where the troops were carried. As the team leader, I was standing on the stepladder high enough to see and direct the pilot to our landing zone. When the chopper was hit and began to fall, I grabbed my weapon and, with a sickened feeling that accompanies desperate anticipation, I moved toward the floor of the cargo area. Before we could hit the ground, the chopper had to crash through the tall trees. The impact was tremendous. Words cannot express the violence of the crash as the chopper landing gear was crushed and the rotor blades broke apart and churned their way through the branches. We were thrown about like marbles in a tin can, and only two of us, the pilot and myself, escaped without serious injury. As our craft came to a grinding stop, there was an odd moment of silence. It was during this brief interlude that I realized the hopelessness of our situation. I could see the extent of the injuries to my team and to the helicopter crew, as most of them could neither walk nor move. I stood to check the pilot, and was relieved to find that he was alive and preparing to help the badly injured co-pilot. We both expected the fuel to burn at any time and, without exchanging words, we anticipated the enemy attack.

The helicopter crew of five consisted of the two pilots, a crew chief, and two door gunners. Door gunners were a fearless breed of soldiers who hung from the doors of the helicopter, firing M60 machine guns. Tragically, many of them returned to the states in cold body bags. Being outside the helicopter during the fall down through the trees, and then during the awful impact, had caused terrible injury to the left-side door gunner. As I worked my way out of the chopper, I heard him moaning loudly. When I turned to help him, he had passed out, and I noticed his right thigh bone protruding through his flesh and clothing. I was certain he was dead. My six-man team included Sgt. Landrum, a big man, and second in command on this mission. I was never on a mission with a better man than Landrum. He had a sprained neck, sprained back, and a dislocated shoulder; but still he was able to carry a weapon and help organize our defense. The rest of my team consisted of four Chinese "Nungs". The Nungs were Chinese mercenaries who lived in South Vietnam and supported Vietnam's democratic government. They were loyal, dedicated and well-trained fighting men. Any one of them would have placed himself in harm's way for me and I was glad to have them along. I had several immediate concerns. First, I expected our position to be over-run, and we would all be killed within an hour. Second, I had to destroy the chopper before we were killed in order to prevent the equipment from falling into the hands of the enemy. And, third, I needed to organize the men for a defensive stand and possible evasion. Although the helicopter would likely burn, I had to rig it for demolition as soon as possible, just in case it did not burn. We usually flew into recon missions at twilight, so we were only minutes from total darkness under the canopy of the jungle. Because of the knowledge I had concerning the special operations of Project Delta, I carried a small .25 caliber automatic handgun. One pull of the trigger delivered four rapid shots. I was to use it on myself, rather than allow myself to be captured and interrogated. Taking one Chinese Nung soldier whose arm was badly broken, I began to search for a final defense position. I found a spot on a small ridge about a hundred yards away from the crash site, and left him at that position to guide me back when I returned with the others. We had a simple nighttime communications procedure consisting of a series of taps on a rifle butt. We would tap three times when approaching a friendly location, and the response would be one tap. This return signal meant we could proceed. If we heard two taps, we immediately stopped. Two taps meant that something was wrong, and that it was not safe for us to approach. On my return to the crash site, I was relieved that the chopper had not started burning. I tapped three times and Landrum gave me one tap in response. The pilot had taken the unconscious co-pilot out and away from the craft. His flak jacket had absorbed the punch of the .51 caliber hit, but the crash landing had left him totally unconscious. I carried another badly injured Nung, while a third Nung with a broken arm walked behind us. The pilot carried the co-pilot, and I led the five of us to the defense position. Still no enemy contact. It was dark now, and I reasoned that if I were the enemy commander, I would move in to surround the wreckage. Once there, I concluded that they wouldn't make contact until morning--an effort to minimize the risk to their own troops. Again leaving these men at the defense position, I quietly moved back to the crash site. While carrying the last wounded Nung, I helped move the helicopter crew chief, who could walk with the help of one of the gunners, to our defense position. By this time, I was feeling the effects of the crash, and was sore and exhausted. When I arrived, Landrum was waiting with the badly injured door gunner. I checked the gunner's pulse, but wasn't sure I could even *detect* a pulse. He had serious internal injuries, and had a badly broken and bloody leg. Even in the dark I could see that he was very pale, and was very likely dead. I had seen plenty of dead. My immediate thought was to leave him where he lay.

A few months earlier, in an equally desperate situation, I had taken the time to locate the body of a Nung, who had been killed on our recon mission. A chopper was coming in to pick up the six of us, but because of the delay caused in carrying the Nung's body out, we were late getting to our pick-up zone. By the time we arrived at this zone, the enemy had set up machine guns and had started shooting at us. Due to intense gunfire they were pouring at the landing zone, I chose not to risk the safety of the helicopter crew and called off our airlift. We happened to be right in the middle of three enemy battalions and were forced to run through enemy locations in our escape attempt. For the next five days, we repeatedly ran into the enemy, and before we could be rescued we had all been seriously wounded. That was a bad experience that may have been avoided if I had not taken the time to carry out the body of the Chinese Nung. Here I was again, with a dead or dying door gunner, in a situation where we would all be dead in a few hours, anyway. For a moment longer I thought of leaving this man, but then I knew that I couldn't. If there *was* a chance for his survival, I had to give it to him. After rigging the chopper with explosives, we set the gunner's broken leg. Landrum held his leg and together we pulled hard until the protruding bone was mostly back in place. We then wrapped his flak jacket around the leg and cinched it tight with the webbing strap from his own safety harness. He did not moan, but remained silent. I was again convinced that he was dead. This was an American soldier, probably a teenager, and whether he was dead or alive, it was only right that he be alongside the rest of us at sunrise. I simply couldn't leave him behind. Too weakened to carry him back up the hill, I dragged him along, as Landrum followed.

At last, totally spent, the three of us joined the others at the top of our little hill. I positioned the pilot on one end of the hill with two automatic weapons, and then positioned Landrum in the middle with most of the grenades. I moved to the other end with two more automatic weapons, while the rest of the wounded--all eight of them--were lined up on the ground between us. To avoid giving the enemy any indication that we had survived the crash, I decided not to destroy the helicopter until the enemy attacked. I had been in some bad circumstances before, but under these conditions, I felt our situation was hopeless. Agonizing moments passed. I then began to hear enemy troop movement and knew that their forces were moving toward us. It was too dark for a Delta team to make a rescue, and because too many of us were wounded, we could not attempt an escape. There were no other A-Teams in our area, and there wasn't a landing zone for miles. We were a handful of wounded men right in the middle of an enemy stronghold, and I could see absolutely no way that we could defend ourselves long enough to be rescued. The pilot was a levelheaded man, and a tremendous moral support to me. I felt sorry for him and his crew. They had not been trained for situations like this, and they fully expected to go home at the end of their tour in Vietnam. I, on the other hand, had *not* expected to survive my tour, and for that reason I seemed to have accepted the situation and my impending death. My sole objective at that point was for us to make a good stand and die doing our honorable best like so many others who had gone before us.

After I set up our defense position, I used my HT-1 radio to try to make contact with the Forward Air Controller (FAC). He was an Air Force Captain who had been a fighter pilot but who was assigned to Delta Project after being grounded for health reasons. His code name was Baron One. He was in an observation aircraft a mile over my head, and was relieved to hear that we were still alive. It was the first contact we had with FAC since being shot down. Baron One used my radio communications to pinpoint our location. I told him that I had the chopper rigged for demolition, but that after the enemy attack in the morning, he should insure its destruction. He was well aware that there was no landing zone in our area, and that we were facing difficult odds. I learned to love that man as he flew overhead the entire night long, leaving only once to refuel. Knowing he was there, and that I could talk to him, made the ordeal somehow bearable. Each radio contact with him was like a prayer. He asked me to be prepared to "show smoke" at first light. Though I did not expect to be alive at first light, I bent over a tall, thin tree and tied a red smoke grenade with a wire that I could pull from the ground.

Many thoughts went through my mind during the next few hours. I thought of my wife, Barbara, and our three sons, Mike, Bobby and Joe. I thought of our tearful goodbye in Montana only six months earlier. I thought of the regrets I had about the marriage problems that had been caused by my service in the Special Forces. Barbara had endured thirteen months of being alone while I was in Korea, then many months alone during my training. Then she had waited at home during my first tour to Vietnam, suffering in a way that only wives can understand, as she lived each day with fear that I had been killed. Now I was gone again for yet another year, and once again this was hard on her and on our marriage. We were growing too far apart and I resigned myself to the fact that we were headed for a divorce. But, how I *loved* her. How sorry I felt that we did not have a normal, happy life. How sorry I was to know that I would never hug my sons again. Oh, how I would miss my sons.

Anticipation of the upcoming attack was enough to drive me to some desperate questions. The government had spent hundreds of thousands of dollars training me. Perhaps I should leave here, with the walking wounded, so I could still be of use to the military? And then the silent, unanswerable questions . . . since it was hopeless anyway, should I take the lives of the men who could not protect themselves in order to prevent their cruel deaths at the hands of the enemy? When the attack did come, I didn't want to die and leave these injured men unable to defend themselves. Since I could not allow myself to be captured, were they better off dying a quiet death in their sleep? Partly to keep myself from losing my mind, and because the moans of the wounded men interfered with my ability to listen for enemy movement, I circled our entire perimeter three times throughout the night. During these patrols, I could hear the enemy concentrated in an area only a couple of hundred yards to the east. My mission was not over. I was there to monitor enemy movement and position, and I did so through the night. I relayed this information to Baron One. Late in the night, the wounded door gunner, who I thought by then would be dead, began to moan. I was almost sorry that this poor man was alive under these conditions. Pushing my thoughts aside, I administered enough morphine to keep him quiet and unconscious through the balance of the night. At the first sign of light, I stirred the men and prepared them for the impending attack. The enemy had started moving toward us, and we braced ourselves for the desperate fight which was about to take place. I knew I had done the right thing to make a stand and die at the side of the wounded men. I had no regrets for having stayed with them.

Even after first light it remained dark under the dense cover of the jungle. Just when the sky was light enough to see, I heard Baron One direct me to pop the smoke grenade. I did so, and informed him that my smoke was red. I heard something and looked up to see fighter aircraft circling over our position. I saw four fighters, then four more, and then four more! The aircraft were loaded with bombs, napalm, and 20mm cannon. Baron One saw my smoke, and over the radio he said, "Hold your heads down, Bobby. We're comin' to get ya." A glimmer of hope raced through each of us. I watched as the first fighter dived towards us, lowering my head just as he dropped a 500-pound bomb directly on the helicopter.

Debris from the explosion rained down all around us. Then came the chilling sound of the fighter jets roaring overhead together with the deafening percussion of the bombs and cannon fire. Glancing toward the wounded door-gunner, I was relieved that I had not left him with that chopper. The remaining fighters made enough terrorizing strafing and bombing runs over the area to completely obliterate the jungle and everything in it. The position of the enemy I had monitored and feared through the night was totally leveled. The "friendly" explosions and cannon fire were so near our locations that we began to fear *them* as much as we feared the enemy. The last two fighters spread napalm fire explosives across that area, and within 10 minutes of my little red smoke signal, there was a landing zone large enough to park a hundred helicopters. As the smoke cleared, Baron One directed me to look to the east. I did so, and saw a half-dozen rescue helicopters with several A-Teams moving into the new, smoking landing zone. The team members, my friends, had us out of there within fifteen minutes. I was too relieved and excited to speak. *All of this for a handful of wounded men...I silently asked myself? Maybe I'll get another chance to make things right with Barbara.*

A few days later, I searched the hospital for the gunner thought to be dead. Miraculously, I found him alive and recovering. Shaking his hands, I nearly collapsed with relief. After all, I had almost left him with the chopper. There had been no tears during that awful night on the jungle hill, but seeing this fellow soldier alive and on his way home unleashed a thousand of them. . . . . .and a thousand since.

18

CHAPTER TWO
Roots

On a beautiful spring morning in March, 1849, a daughter was born to a Blackfeet Indian woman and her French-fur-trapper husband, Charles Choquette. The girl, named Malenda, was very intelligent, and at the age of eight was taken by her father to Peoria, Illinois. It was there that she learned to speak English and was educated in the ways of the white people. Malenda, living in Abraham Lincoln's home state, was sixteen years old when the President was assassinated. Even as a very old woman she could vividly recall the events of that fateful day as the people in Illinois felt the terrible loss of the President. At the age of seventeen, she returned to her Indian people, and accepted employment as an interpreter for the Blackfeet Indian Nation, a stewardship she would have for the rest of her life. Her people lived life in the old ways, fighting battles with other tribes and with the white people. In 1867, at the young age of eighteen, Malenda married a frontiersman named George Samuel Wren. Twenty-one years and eleven children later, she gave birth to a son whom she named William Wren. William grew to manhood among the Blackfeet people, and eventually married a Canadian girl named Ella Kihn. Ella was the daughter of German immigrants who farmed land next to the border of the Blackfeet Indian Reservation. William, born in 1888, is my Blackfeet Indian father, and Ella, born in 1911, is my German mother. I was born on September 29, 1938, in a small house on the Blackfeet Indian Reservation. The Reservation is adjacent to Glacier National Park in Montana. I have wonderful and fond memories of my youthful days on the reservation. The spectacular beauty of the land is matched only by the vicious cold of the winters. As a young Indian boy I walked two miles each morning to school. Rain, shine, snow, below zero--it didn't matter. I did not even think about it. That was just the way things were. The school kids at our one-room elementary school on the reservation took turns with the assignment to arrive early enough and get the pot-belly stove started to heat up the schoolroom. I often walked through the dark morning, in the bitter cold, with only a jacket to protect me from the elements. Since those early days, I have often watched the cattle and horses standing out in the pastures, probably frozen stiff, and wondered if the Blackfeet school children are still walking through the cold with ragged coats. I have many memories of growing up on the reservation. A few stand out and are worth repeating. I recall being quite young and sitting on the lap of my Blackfeet grandmother, Malenda, and looking into her aged, wrinkled eyes. She was very old, and I was only three, but I distinctly remember knowing and feeling of her love. I just *knew* she loved me. It was Grandma who had named me. She always spoke to me in her native Blackfeet language, while my grandmother Kihn spoke to me in her native German tongue. I remember many family trips, by horse and wagon, traveling five miles across the Canadian border to visit Grandma and Grandpa Kihn. They always made me feel loved and welcome. I was happy as an Indian boy with German blood, and I have very warm feelings as I recall those days. As a young boy, I was given the Indian name of Keepippokayo. The name means 'Many Bears', and I was raised to carry the name proudly.

The winter weather in northern Montana is terribly unforgiving. Occasionally we would be snowbound out on the plains in our small homes and sometimes would run out of firewood. I remember my brother Bill and I cutting down a power pole and chopping it for fire fuel. In the winter of 1945, when I was just seven years old, my father, William, and my younger brother, Jerry, became very ill with pneumonia. One night my mother was up late, desperately trying to provide the proper care for them. She treated their terrible fevers as well as she knew how, but late that night both my father and little brother Jerry silently passed away. In her sorrow, mother wrapped herself in blankets then walked through a blizzard to the neighboring ranch to obtain help. Before leaving her home, she stoked the wood stove hot enough to keep my older brother, Bill, and myself, warm while she was gone. A short time later, when returning home, she found our house burning. She had stoked the fire too hot and caused a house fire. Grief-stricken, frozen, and now panicked, she rushed into the house and fought the flames to protect her two surviving sons. She was able to distinguish the flames before the house was lost, but she later confessed that if she had been alone, with no other children to care for, she might have simply given up in her grief and died in the fire. Although that fateful night was a half century ago, it is still an emotional experience for mother to speak of. She worked hard, was faithful, and never failed to show her love and devotion to her children. In the very worst of my days, and during my greatest struggles, it was my mother who was there to hold me in her arms and comfort me.

Mom could have kept out of financial trouble if she

hadn't been a white widow in Indian country, and if she hadn't been burdened with a very labor-intensive sheep ranch to tend. In spite of her burdens, however, she handled herself well, and won the respect of the tribesmen who planned to take her ranch from her. Some of our Indian relatives were jealous of a white woman having such good land, and she finally asked the tribal council to help her sell the property. Eventually, she would make a new life somewhere else.

After my father and younger brother died, big brother Bill and I were alone with mother on our small ranch. We didn't mean to be such troublemakers, it was just that the reservation was not an easy life. Nor was it a place to learn social graces and etiquette. It didn't take long before Bill and I started getting into trouble. One afternoon a neighboring rancher, a large, mean Indian called Angus, paid us an unexpected visit. He was madder than the devil about our mongrel dog, Rover, killing one of his sheep. He had already warned us to keep Rover away from his ranch. On this particular afternoon, he came to see us with a gun. Without hesitation, he took Rover over to the side of the barn and, right in front of us, he shot and killed our dog Rover. We were devastated by this act of cruelty, but we were only six and ten years old and had little chance of stopping him. That same night, however, we thought of a way to even the score. After getting some matches, we walked the five or six miles to the Angus' ranch, and lit his haystack on fire. The blaze lit up the sky for miles. The next day he came by to whip each of us, but Uncle John, our dad's brother, was there to defend us. Uncle John was a big mean Indian himself, and stared at Angus as he said, "You shot their dog, they burned your hay.

Now go home...it's over."

Some time after this, Bill and I finally pushed mom over the edge with our pranks. Although I did not realize it at the time, we were poor folks. Often we ate simple meals like a mixture of flour and molasses. Perhaps that is part of the reason that we came up with creative ways to get some money in our hands. Bill and I had a bad habit of waiting for mom to go to sleep, then sneaking out of the house and going into town. We had thought of a new method of getting a little spending money, and wanted to try it out. By this time, Bill was a man-sized thirteen-year old, and I was only nine, but neither of us was afraid of anything. We knew of an alley that had a back door to a saloon where an occasional drunken Indian would wander out. We figured the drunks would have a few dollars, so we went to the alley and waited. Our plan worked perfectly. Bill stood behind the door, which was up a flight of five or six steps. My heart was beating like a war-drum when finally a drunkard walked out and shut the door. As he turned, Bill clenched his fist and clobbered the drunk on the back of the head as hard as he could, and knocked him down the steps. Before the man could recover, I reached for his wallet and we made our escape. We knew full well that in his condition he could not catch us. We had learned our manners on the reservation, and had been raised in a climate where it was considered a mark of manhood to take things from white men and drunk Indians. The man had a roll of cash that nearly burst my eyes. Being older, and in charge of things, Bill kept the lion's share of the cash while convincing me that it was an even split. Anyway, with my $40 share of the money, I was eager to buy candy and spend this money as quickly, although as recklessly, as I could.

We may have walked away clean from our misdeed, except for one thing - only a few days prior to stealing our fortune, someone had robbed the town Western Union office. The sheriff was on the lookout for the suspects when he got word that a couple of half-breed kids from outside of town were spending a lot of money. I noticed the sheriff's car parked at our house that afternoon, but I wasn't bright enough to think that Bill and I were in trouble. I walked right into the house, my pockets full of money, and my mouth full of candy. It wasn't until I saw the look on Bill's face that it dawned on me that the sheriff was there to ask us a few questions. We decided to take the rap for the Western Union robbery because we were both afraid to tell mom the truth, that we had rolled a drunk at three in the morning. It was the last straw for mother and she agreed with the judge to send us to a boarding school. Mom sold the farm to her brothers, and complied with the judge by enrolling Bill and me in the Deaconess School for Boys, in Helena, Montana. At the time, I didn't understand the financial struggle mother was having. She took a job in a laundry and was working twelve-hour days, sometimes seven days a week, to support our family and keep us in school. We were both angry with her during those next two years. Although she visited us often, we hated the school and the terribly strict discipline enforced there. Even so, being in such a strict environment was the best thing that could have happened to us. I later discovered that discipline is one of the most important and indispensable elements of life. It was at this school that I learned to be obedient and to work hard, or face the 'rubber-shoeing'.

Although I never had to face the rubber shoe, I watched other kids be beat by the sole of a boot and determined to follow the rules to avoid that punishment.

Shortly after our release from the boy's school, our mother married a man named J.J. Galbreath. He was a Blackfeet Indian who had a position as a Tribal Councilman and was very helpful to mother as she arranged for the sale of the ranch. My new stepfather, JJ, was a Mormon man. I didn't exactly know what that meant and really did not care, but mother told us it meant he was special. JJ had been converted to the LDS church by a prominent Mormon man named James E. Talmage and then became a good influence for the Mormon church on the Blackfeet Reservation. Mom joined his church and took us there to get baptized. Bill and I had no interest in religious things and accepted the baptism, but without commitment. We attended the Mormon meetings on Sunday, sometimes held in the bowling alley in Cut Bank, Montana, and I can remember the folks there trying to teach me of spiritual things. My mother had two more children, Suell and Kin Jay. I was a teenager as my little sister and brother were growing up and we became very close. My stepfather proved himself to be a good man as he cared for our family and was a good influence on Bill and myself. We began to function as a family and had a few wonderful years. However, my mother would soon grieve again. JJ developed Muscular Dystrophy and died in 1959. In her short years she had already buried two husbands and a son.

Bill and I spent our high school years in the small farming community of Hamilton, Montana. We were better behaved after having spent those two years at the Boys School, but our etiquette still required polishing. That is, until I met Barbara Callender. I had never really had a girlfriend before. I was a half-breed Indian boy with all the charm of a rutting buffalo, so why would this white cheerleader have the slightest interest in *me*? I couldn't answer that, but still she did. I first noticed Barbara when she sneezed and blew her nose in class. *That is a beautiful girl*, I thought, as our eyes made contact for the very first time. Barbara and I soon became acquainted, and as high school courtships go, it was not long before we were meeting each other's parents. I became a new person. The emptiness I had felt in my heart for so many years, but had not understood, had finally been filled. I was consumed by images of this beautiful cheerleader. I loved her like I had never loved before. What's more, I knew *she* loved me. Before long, we realized we had no further desire to remain single. I had purchased a '49 Ford, for $100.00, and was in the process of customizing it at the time of our marriage. It had purple-colored primer paint, and "frenched" headlights. I was the proudest Indian in Montana. With our parents' support, we drove 90 miles to Salmon, Idaho, where we were married by a Presbyterian minister in a small church there. The date was April 21, 1956. Barbara's parents, Louis and Maybelle Callender, as well as her sister and her husband, were there to lend their support, and we couldn't have been happier. Of our marriage, Barbara adds: "For my wedding dress, I wore a delicate pink linen suit with white piping, and off we went to Salmon, Idaho. Because I was Presbyterian, I insisted on being married in the Presbyterian . church. Although Bob was LDS, his membership in that church was 'in name only,' so he acquiesced to my wishes. I was excited to begin this new phase of my young life! I loved Bob, I had confidence in him, and I knew I could trust him to be a faithful companion. He would take good care of me, and although the challenge of meeting our financial obligations seemed insurmountable, still we knew we could work together and manage without help. While we were really in love, we were still only kids, and in some ways we acted like kids! After the wedding ceremony at the church, my parents took some snapshots of us, then left for home. Bob and I had a shrimp dinner at a modest restaurant, then attended the western movie *Tall in the Saddle*. We held hands during the movie, and we both felt as if we would never know unhappiness!" Following a three-day honeymoon in Salmon, Barbara and I left t high school and we moved to an apartment in Missoula, Montana. Barbara finished her senior year of high school there by correspondence. Throughout this year, I worked at a Firestone garage, then at a railroad yard that was five miles across town. Barbara was driving through town one afternoon and upon seeing some of her friends, she waved and did not notice the stop sign, nor the car which hit her and ruined my personalized, customized, pride and joy, 1949 Ford. She was not injured, but felt badly about the ruined car. Since we had no other transportation, I walked to work at the Firestone Garage each day. Later I got work at the railroad with much better pay, but it was a ten-mile round trip each day, on foot. We had little money, so each morning I ate a hearty meal of pancakes, then went without eating until arriving home again in the evening.

On November 30, 1956, our first son, Michael, was

born. Even under our humble circumstances, those were wonderful days as Mike became the light of our lives. Of this special time, Barbara states: "The months before Mike was born were happy, almost carefree for us. We were too young and inexperienced to be worried, least of all about money or our future. We saved our money in a sock, and we would often pour it out and count it. After all, we had to have enough saved to pay for our baby, a bill that totaled $150. On the day that Mike was born, my doctor advised me to take castor oil in grape juice in order to induce labor. This potion worked, and before long Bob came home from work and drove me to St. Patrick's Hospital. When we arrived Bob was ushered into a waiting room and I was then taken into the delivery room where Mike soon was born. Never had I felt so fulfilled, as I felt the joy of being a mother and the thrill of having our son safely with us was beyond words. We loved him before he was born, and even more afterward when we could touch his little fingers and toes, and hold him near our hearts. Bob was an excellent father, and we went about the work of parenting without fear." Barbara and I had dreams and ambitions that outweighed reality; but still we had hopes of a special life together with our tiny son. I dreamed of doing well financially, and having the money to provide nice things for my little family. I soon learned how difficult it would be to earn an income enough for our needs. The following year, in an effort to improve our condition, I joined the National Guard. I found these few extra dollars each month to be a great benefit. Because Barbara had gotten into an accident with our only car, I purchased two more automobiles. The first, a '31 Model A Ford Sedan convertible, was canary yellow, and cost about $25. I also paid $35 for a '29 Model

A Ford that had been spray-painted a lavender color. One day, when I returned home from work, little one-year-old Mike was crying loudly. I took him into my arms, walked outside, and showed him the yellow convertible. It must have been a hit because every evening thereafter I would return home to find Mike ready to jump again into my arms demanding that I show him the car.

On May 6, 1958, our second son, Bobby, was born. Barbara was 18 years old, and I was 19. Medical expenses had increased since our first son's birth, and Bobby's arrival cost us a whopping $200. With our family growing and our income entirely inadequate, I had decided to join the Army full-time. Besides having greater income, this would enable us to have health benefits. So, on May 10, 1958, only four days after Bobby was born, I left for Basic Training. Barbara adds: "The day I was released from the hospital after having Bobby, we traveled 100 miles to my parent's home, where I was to stay with our two little ones. This was a very uncomfortable trip, given my condition, and I was greatly relieved to finally arrive at our destination. The following morning, Bob left for Fort Ord, California, to begin his military career. Basic Training lasted eight weeks, and what a lonely eight weeks this was. When he returned, we took a short leave to visit his mother who had moved to Provo, Utah. Afterward, we headed for Fort Chaffee, Arkansas, our first Army base. Because he was still in training, I had to live off Base with the boys; so he and I could only visit each evening for 15 to 20 minutes. This lonely routine lasted four months, at which time Bob received orders for overseas duty in Korea. He was so hesitant in telling me of his 13-month assignment in Korea, without us, that I didn't learn of his destination until after he had helped me and the boys get settled in to stay with my mother and father at their home in Anaconda, Montana. I can still feel the shock of that news! It was devastating to me, and of course a very difficult thing for Bob. Our world had really crashed in around us. Even though there wasn't an active war going on in Korea at this time, still I worried about him continuously. I wrote to him every day for 365 days" The next thirteen months were long and difficult for both of us. I spent them on duty near the South Korean Demilitarized Zone which is the border between North and South Korea. On May Day of 1959, I was standing guard at the DMZ. As Sergeant of the Guard, I was up in an observation tower when bursts of machinegun fire startled me. When the bullets rattled the tower, I became, for the first time, a target of enemy fire. It would not be the last. I spent the rest of that year doing my duty. I also spent considerable time studying, receiving a high school diploma, and even earning some college credits. One day a young lieutenant aggravated me to the point of confrontation with him. He reported his bloody nose and blackened eye to the company commander and I was disciplined and charged with the offense. The Army took half of my pay for several months that put a terrible financial strain on us. I learned my lesson and never beat up an officer again.

My tearful and long-anticipated reunion with Barbara and the boys, after more than a year of separation, took place in December of 1959. I flew back to the states, then Barbara met me at the Salt Lake International Airport. It was especially gratifying for us as we spent the next four days honeymooning at the Temple Square Motel, in Salt Lake City. We visited local sites, and just enjoyed being back together. We then drove home to Montana and the boys. Oh, how I loved this beautiful woman at my side, and how she fulfilled my needs. Being together again with her, and then with our little sons, was like a dream from which I hoped never to awaken.

Upon my return to duty, I was stationed for one year at Fort Hood, Texas. We moved to Texas as a family, and soon found that we were expecting our third son. We decided to name him Joe David. His birth was a belated Christmas present, and took place on the evening of December 27, 1960. By this time, Mike was five, and Bobby was three. Barbara spent her days being a happy full-time Mom. As a family we had never had it so good.

CHAPTER THREE
The Green Beret

With the exception of having beat up an officer, I was a good soldier, I worked very hard, and I wanted to excel in a military career. One day an announcement was circulated that a military unit, known as the Special Forces, was looking for volunteers. The training was supposed to be very difficult, but if a soldier could successfully endure it, he would qualify for an unusual, but prestigious round hat. It was known as the Green Beret. I applied for, and was accepted, into the training program for this elite group of soldiers. I had a natural aptitude for mathematics, so my test scores helped me immensely. Barbara and I relocated with our children to Fort Bragg, North Carolina where I began a training program that would span the next six years.

Medical Training was first on the list. I remember thinking I would learn how to use bandages and take blood pressures, but the Special Forces had a different idea of medical training, and before I was through, I was qualified to perform surgical operations on wounded men under extreme combat conditions. This training began with twenty weeks of anatomy and basic medical training at Ft. Sam Houston, near San Antonio, Texas. I was fortunate to have Barbara and the boys there with me. During the few breaks we were given, I took the family to the beach in Corpus Christi, boating trips on local lakes, and across the border into Mexico. This time with my family still ranks as one of my happiest memories. There were a few out of our class who failed the first phase of medical training, but those who passed were sent to Fort

Benning, Georgia for four additional weeks of surgical training. We assisted in surgical procedures, and learned a great deal by watching and being coached by the surgeons. The true test, however, was yet to come. We were next sent to Ft. Bragg, North Carolina, for the Special Forces 'Dog Lab'. This consisted of sixteen weeks of very intensive surgical training. We were trained by a doctor who was highly qualified in every aspect of medical and surgical procedures. During the final few weeks of the Dog Lab, our surgeon, Dr. Huey, required each of us to anesthetize a dog and then shoot a bullet into its right rear leg. Each of us took turns on his own dog, acting the part of the chief surgeon, while the others took their turns as scrub nurse, assistant surgeon or anesthetist. I surgically removed the bullet from my dog, taking care to control the bleeding and carefully stitching the wound. I knew that if my dog died, I would fail the entire school. After successfully nursing my dog back to health, Dr. Huey asked me to perform an amputation of the same leg. I anesthetized the dog, carefully monitoring its heartbeat and blood pressure, then amputated the leg using the same surgical procedures which would be expected if the patient had been human. Dr. Huey watched over my shoulder; and after I successfully performed the surgery, he gave me a 'pop quiz'. He asked me to find a certain nerve in the dog's front shoulder, then surgically follow it all the way to the dog's paw. I was not to allow any profuse bleeding, and had to tie off all blood vessels as well as keep the dog alive. Somehow I was given the insight to accomplish this, and upon successfully completing the operation and the quiz, Dr. Huey gave me passing marks. Of the ninety trainees who had started the class at Sam Houston, only fourteen of us qualified as Special Forces medics. This training would soon be used under difficult circumstances. I would like to note that the dogs' lives were sacrificed for the purpose of training men to *save human lives*. I do not advocate the use of animals in this manner, except in the most critical of circumstances. Once in combat, we were called upon to use the knowledge we had gained in training. One of our Special Forces medics even had to amputate his own wounded leg, under combat conditions, in order to save his own life. The rest of us used our training on many occasions to do what we were trained to do . . . that is, save human lives.

Barbara reflects on this time, and on her growing concerns: "During this period of training, Bob would be gone for sometimes weeks at a time. Even when he was home, he often *wasn't*. He was under great pressure, and always wanted to do everything perfectly, and be the best he could be. Even so, very often after I'd planned a meal from early in the day, Bob would not be home until very early the next morning. His plate would be left on the dining room table."

Following our medical training, we spent the next fourteen weeks in very intense physical and psychological training. This regimentation included sixteen hours per day, for seven days a week. Our schedules also included 'guidance training', which was administered by a chaplain who admonished us to live high moral standards. I had originally joined the Army to help provide for my family, so when I went to Airborne school and received my jump wings, I was tickled clear through to find out that I was paid an extra $55 each month for 'jump pay'. To Barbara and I, this additional income seemed like a fortune. I still remember jokingly telling her that I would have jumped *without* a parachute for that much money.

A Special Forces A-Team consisted of a 12-man unit that was specially trained in guerilla warfare and covert operations and tactics. We were shown how a 1960 incident in Lebanon might have been avoided by the training we were receiving. My training included French and Chinese language instruction. It also included a segment on Vietnamese history, geography, traditions and customs. We were taught the proper use of explosives for demolition, and were taught engineering principles for building "something out of nothing." We learned to navigate with a compass, with maps, or by stars; and to pinpoint our location on maps within minutes, day or night. Everything we did during those months was together as an A-Team. We were continually on mock guerilla exercises where we would parachute into an area, execute a mission, then return to a pick-up location. After each mission, we attended a debriefing session, during which we would question each member of our team about every detail of the mission. We critiqued one another until we knew each other's character and response, and we could anticipate how each team member would describe a mission. One team member might ask the others on his team what kind of trees were in a particular area. If we didn't each know the answer that time, we would after the *next* mission. It was the same for knowing the height of specific trees, the types of soil and rocks in a given area, etc. That kind of training continued until we all knew the answer to every detailed question about every mission.

I was still a few weeks away from graduation as a qualified member of the Special Forces when we received word that President Kennedy was coming to Ft. Bragg to witness a demonstration of a Special Forces operation. The President was a tremendous supporter of the Special Forces, and asked that he personally award the Green Beret to an A-Team. On short notice, twelve of us were selected for this unusual assignment, and on October 31, 1961, John Fitzgerald Kennedy, President of the United States of America, stood in front of me and shook my hand. Then, with a warm smile, he awarded me the highly coveted Green Beret. This ceremony took place on Barbara's twenty-second birthday. She was there in attendance and felt as if she were receiving the award right along with me for all the sacrifice she had made to rear our sons while I earned the right to wear the green beret.

I was assigned to an A-Team in November 1961, and continued the same grueling training pace. My A-Team was fortunate enough to have some particularly realistic training. During the Fall of 1962, our Commander-In-Chief, President Kennedy, had a disagreement with the Russians. The Soviet Union had begun to build nuclear missile bases in Cuba, and this led to what has become known as the 'Cuban Missile Crisis'. Our Special Forces units were asked to prepare for missions to destroy those missile bases. We trained day and night for weeks in preparation, and on a night in late October, 1962, I was on a C-130 aircraft as a member of an A-Team. We had orders to locate and destroy one of those missile bases. The mission included ten A-Teams, five of which would start the mission, with five other teams in reserve. The reserve teams had precisely the same instructions as the first teams, and were to be called upon if the first teams were killed before destroying the missile bases. I was on one of the first teams. Our mission was clear, and we were fully prepared. At 9:00 one night, we were flying off the north shore of Cuba with orders to begin our mission at midnight. That was the deadline hour set by President Kennedy for the Russians to back down, or to face war. I suppose each of us was thinking the same thoughts over the next couple of hours. I thought of our mission--over and over again. I thought of my family, and whether I would ever see them again. I thought of death, and what it might be like. At 11:00 that night we were relieved, yet strangely disappointed, when we were notified that the Soviet Union had agreed to remove their missiles from Cuba. Our mission was canceled. I am not at liberty to provide the actual details of the mission, but a few days later we arrived at Ft. Bragg, and I was home in time for Barbara's twenty-third birthday.

The mock missions continued as we were becoming more and more prepared for live ones. We became much more somber about our training when we received orders that our team had three months to prepare for a mission in Vietnam. I knew it was time and that I was prepared to put my life on the line, yet never could I have imagined the full impact of the horrors of war that awaited me over the next several years.

Special Forces Prayer

Almighty GOD, who art the Author of Liberty
and the champion of the oppressed, hear our prayer.

We, the men of the Special Forces, acknowledge our
dependence upon Thee in the preservation of human
freedom.

Go with us as we seek to defend the defenseless and to
free the enslaved.

May we ever remember that our nation, whose motto is
"In God We Trust", expects that we shall acquit
ourselves with honor, that we may never bring shame
upon our faith, our families, or our fellow men.

Grant us wisdom from Thy hand, courage from Thine
heart, strength from thine arm, and protection from
thine hand.

It is for Thee that we do battle, and to thee belongs the
victor's crown. For Thine is the Kingdom, and the
power and the glory, forever, AMEN.

Dear Daddy,

A few weeks ago you left with the other men in green hats. I watched you and those men smile and wave as you got on the airplane. I was worried when I saw all the mom's crying because they said you were going to a war. Are you afraid? Because I was. I kept having bad dreams that a tank would run over you and you would get killed. It scared me. The night you left I started thinking about God, so I got out of bed and kneeled down and asked him to keep you alive no matter what happened. I prayed and then I cried and then I did it again every night until last night. I feel better now, because I know God will keep you alive. He promised me that you won't die.

Love,

Mike

CHAPTER FOUR
Vietnam, 1963

Telling Barbara that we would be separated again was one of the hardest things I ever did. Tears flowed freely. We both knew that I was going to a war zone, and her tears were accompanied by the pressing question of what would she do without me...if I didn't come home alive? Of this time, Barbara states: "The night before Bob left for his first tour in Vietnam, we lay sideways across the bedspread together, holding hands, and crying softly. We were both so full of pain that we couldn't even talk about it. We loved each other very much. Late the next day, the boys and I drove to Pope Air Force Base to see Bob off and to say our goodbyes with the other wives and families. I brought our movie camera along, and filmed some of the other soldiers and their families.

Then, after a tearful farewell, I filmed Bob and the others boarding the huge plane bound for Vietnam. Bob was wearing his fatigue uniform, highly shined boots and the green beret that he had worked so hard to earn. He carried a large pack on his back, and looked very handsome and adventurous. But the boys and I weren't thinking of that, as much as we were the pain in our hearts for seeing him go. In addition, I was paralyzed with fear for his well-being. Dusk had fallen when I filmed his plane as it took off from the tarmac. My camera followed it up into the darkening sky until at last it disappeared, leaving only the full moon to keep me company. I then turned, took our boys' hands, and headed for the car and our trip home . . . only to wait."

Our flight was uneventful, and at last we touched down at the military air base near Saigon. Once in the country, we boarded a C-130 and then flew on to a place called Da Lat. It was located in the southern highlands of the II Corps area, about 200 miles northeast of Saigon. From there, we were transported by trucks to a remote settlement known as Dijirai (Didg-yer-eye). This place was inhabited by native mountain people, whom the earlier French forces called the 'Montagnards', but whom the American troops nick-named Mountain Yards. These Montagnards were mostly uneducated people, and it was our mission to help organize them into a community capable of resisting enemy communist forces. At that time, there was at least as much combat trouble from unorganized renegade bands from South Vietnam, as there was from organized North Vietnamese soldiers. Our mission was to build a military post and organize an Army from the Montagnard people. We even had the finances to provide a payroll to those volunteers who helped during the construction of the camp, as well as to pay those who volunteered as soldiers. There were other A-Team camps all over South Vietnam doing the same things that we were doing. The military units we were training were known as the Civilian Irregular Defense Group (CIDG, pronounced sid-gee). We had been taught to speak enough of the Vietnamese language that communication was little or no problem; but we were also fortunate to have found an English-speaking Frenchman who lived near Dijirai, and who operated a tobacco farm there. He was very helpful in teaching us more of the Vietnamese language and local customs. Twelve of us were dropped off at this settlement--with no friends, no sleeping area, and little food. We were given the task of making friends and soldiers out of simple people who had no idea who we were, or why we were there. With the help of about a hundred natives, we spent the next six weeks constructing an A-Team camp. We chose a relatively level piece of ground, and completely cleared an area of over ten acres. The jungle vegetation was thick, and the labor was difficult, but we found that the men and the women were willing to work for pay.

As the days sped into weeks, I was greatly relieved to receive letters from home. Barbara was her usual cheery self, but I could tell she missed me, and that she still loved me. I also received letters from our sons, and I could tell Barbara had helped them put together their thoughts.

In the early days of our team's assignment in Vietnam, there were very few helicopters to fly in with supplies. Still, we were able to call for parachute airdrops. We utilized the density of the local timber as much as possible, and had other supplies dropped in to us. Because we were periodically fired upon by unknown forces, we felt an increasing urgency to complete the camp construction. During the day we would take time to teach classes on democracy, simple medical care, and sanitation. Then, during the night, we would attend the Montagnard feasts and occasional buffalo sacrifices. We built a dam up the river and diverted clean water through hand-dug canals in order to allow it to flow through our camp and provide water for cooking, cleaning and sanitation. Inside the camp, we constructed our sleeping quarters, a mess hall and a hospital. As the camp medic, I delivered babies, and treated civilian injuries; and became rather popular among the natives. Many of these people had been infected with a serious rash on their lower legs. I prescribed penicillin, which worked absolute wonders on nearly every affliction they had, except the rash. I tried antibiotic ointments, bandages and everything I could think of to heal this rash but without success, until finally I discovered that streptomycin would clear it up in just a few days. I called for more airdrops of medical supplies, and reported the success of the streptomycin to medical personnel back in the states. As a result, they supplied other A-Team camps with the same medication for the natives in other areas, and it was not long before the streptomycin solution was widespread and popular among the natives of Vietnam.

We recruited about two hundred Montagnards as soldiers, and trained them daily in basic combat tactics. They were willing to learn, and were also willing to face the enemy. It was during the fourth month of this training that the enemy attacks began to intensify. Our patrols were regularly ambushed, and we decided it was time to retaliate and go on the offensive. The patrols were no longer just for reconnaissance, but were designed to find the enemy and drive them off. These missions became more and more dangerous, but they were very valuable in giving us experience, and served to purify the ranks of the Special Forces. It is difficult to know how a soldier will react in an intense combat situation. He can be trained and prepared as well as the next man, but 'under fire' his true colors will show through. I knew hundreds of soldiers who qualified to wear the Green Beret, but I knew of only one who was removed from the ranks of the Special Forces. In June of 1963, I led an expedition of three platoons to find the enemy and drive them from our area. Each platoon had about thirty Montagnards, with an A-Team leader in charge. My platoon was in the lead, with another platoon about a hundred yards to my left. The third platoon was held in reserve, about two hundred yards to my rear. An A-Team leader, whom I will refer to as Sergeant Red, was in charge of the reserve unit. Late in the afternoon of the second day, my platoon was ambushed and was taking gunfire from our front. This was exactly what we were looking for, so I called for the platoon to my left to move into an offensive position and together we would assault the location of the enemy ambush. Just as we began our counter-attack, I was surprised by another enemy ambush from our rear. I remember thinking what a great tactic the enemy had used, and I vowed to try it--*if* I got out of this alive. I was now taking fire from two sides, but decided to continue the frontal assault and call on the reserve platoon to come forward and attack the enemy that had surprised me from the rear. I radioed to Sergeant Red, but had no answer. My first thought was that he had been ambushed and killed, and that his platoon of Montagnards was in disarray. I had little choice but to split my platoon and assault in two directions--both front and rear. I barked out the orders to my Montagnard platoon and they followed my instructions closely. Instead of fighting from our ambushed position, we mounted a fierce attack, in two directions. This plan worked, and the enemy retreated; but not before eight of my men were wounded. Still concerned for Sergeant Red and his platoon, I led two squads to the area where he should have been; but we could find no sign of them. After treating the bloodied and wounded men, I radioed back to the base camp and asked if they had any communications with Sergeant Red. During that conversation, Red came running into base camp, with his platoon behind him, and announced the deaths of the rest of us. He had panicked and retreated in the face of enemy fire. The ground that we had taken almost two days to patrol was covered in three hours of his hasty retreat. Every soldier in the camp was embarrassed with this sergeant's action. As I stitched up my wounded men, I swore that I would never run or shrink in the face of enemy fire, and I would never allow anyone else to show that awful disgrace to the badge we called the Green Beret.

Because we had no helicopter support, there was no chance to evacuate the wounded. Therefore, I dressed their wounds and we continued our mission. We still had three days of our mission to complete and I intended to do so. If the injuries had been more serious, I could have sent a squad back with the wounded. However, since we were already short one platoon, and we knew the enemy was in the area, I decided to keep both remaining platoons together and care for the wounded while continuing the patrol. The next few days of patrol were uneventful. When we finally arrived back at the base camp, I found that Sergeant Red had already been taken back to headquarters for an investigation of the incident. I was called on to present the evidence as I saw it, and Sergeant Red was removed from the Special Forces. It was a dark day for our team.

By August, the enemy ambushes had partially subsided, and our camp was fully operational. We had a reasonably well-trained army of Montagnards, we had a well-supplied hospital, and we had completed our mission. Within two weeks, we received orders to return to Ft. Bragg. My flight schedule leaving Vietnam included a flight in a C-123 Provider plane from Saigon, to a place called Can Tho, about 150 miles south of Saigon. On our way to Can Tho, we stopped briefly in the small town of Vihn Long. On our departure from Vihn Long--just as we got into the air at the end of the runway--our plane was hit by machine gun fire. The engines were knocked out, and we began to plummet to the ground. There was little I could do except sit and hope for the best. The pilot reacted well, and did a marvelous job of gliding us to a controlled crash landing. We hit the ground hard, destroying 2000 feet of rice paddy before coming to a stop--and all without any serious injuries. The enemy who moved into position with their machine gun were the epitome of guerilla warfare. They moved in, shot down our plane, and moved out, all within less than an hour-- and nobody ever knew who they were, or where they went.

Within a week I was home again with Barbara and the kids. I had been gone for six months, and I couldn't have been more relieved to be safely home again. My family was relieved, as well, and when I shared my experiences with them, we all knew I had been blessed with special protection. Shortly after my return home, I took a long leave with the family. We took a trip to Washington D.C., and saw the great monuments and historical sites of our country. We rode a ferryboat and enjoyed the porpoises and sea turtles that swam alongside. It was truly a wonderful reunion. Later we went on a family camping trip to the Blue Ridge Mountains. The scenery was beautiful, the company was wonderful, and the memories of that trip are still clear. But, after all the intense situations I had been through--from the Cuba mission to Vietnam--I was surprised to find myself threatened by the bureaucracy of the good old United States. While enjoying a pancake breakfast at our Blue Ridge Mountain camp, a forest ranger drove by and saw me clip a twig from a tree. I had just finished clearing acres of trees in a war zone, and I had no idea that, in a U.S. Forest, cutting shrubs was considered a crime. The ranger nearly threw me in jail with a threat to fine me hundreds of dollars...simply because I had clipped that twig. I listened patiently and promised him that I would never again cause such destruction of the forest. He finally settled down and dismissed the charges. Must have been a special tree. In spite of this, our family vacation was therapeutic for all of us, and as I prepared to resume my responsibilities in the Special Forces, I would fall back on these memories for years to come.

Dear Daddy,

I was so glad when you came home from the war. It was fun to see you some more. I tell all my friends that you are a Green Beret and that President Kennedy gave it to you but some of them don't believe me. Mom says you're learning more things about being a good soldier. We miss you. When you're finished can you take us camping again? I am in second grade now. Last week we went to the demonstration that the other Green Berets did and it was neat. They showed guns and bombs and there were paratroopers too. I am proud of what you do. Come home soon.

Love,

Mike

CHAPTER FIVE
The Closing Doors

There was never a point when a Green Beret soldier could be pronounced 'completely trained'. Our breed of soldier could not look forward to a time when he had learned all there was to learn, and could then relax and work regular hours. There were enough different training courses available that a man could put in his twenty years, in training, and retire without repeating a single class. And so it was that I spent the next eighteen months in one training program after another. Although the stress of my profession was affecting my family more and more, still I wanted to do anything I could to be a good husband and father. I had no greater desire. As previously mentioned, I was only eighteen years old when Barbara and I were married. Back then we had few concerns.

I had loads of friends, worked hard to earn a living, and really did not worry about *anything*. In those days, I was like a puppy that played and played with little or no thought of serious things. Part of that 'puppy syndrome' faded with age, but a much larger part faded with the experience of war. I was a different person now. I was more somber, less playful, more serious, and less fun. I thought more carefully about decisions I made, and I thought more deeply about life and death. It was ferociously clear to me that I was being trained to serve military missions that would place me in life and death, kill or be killed, situations. War changes men.

Even so, I had very personal motives for staying in the Special Forces. In the first place, I truly felt that what I did was important to my country. We were trained for missions to defend our country, and to free the oppressed. This two-prong mission statement gave me a tremendous sense of honor. I was no longer only a half-breed Indian kid. I had earned the rare privilege of wearing the Green Beret, and had become a member of the finest fighting force in the world. This sense of belonging was increasingly euphoric, and even though I expected that my continued service in the Special Forces would find me in another war zone, and would likely result in my death, I could not and *would not* walk away.

Furthermore, where would I go? I had trained to be a soldier, and had trained for nothing else. I had a beautiful wife and three sons who were well housed, well fed, and who had free health care. The security of steady paychecks was very valuable for my peace of mind. There was really no decision to make. I would stay the course, and would trust my fate in the hands of God. Barbara had supported me through the last seven years of our marriage. She had waited while I went to

Korea for 13 months, she had waited while I went away for months and months of training, she had waited for months while we secretly trained for the Cuba invasion, and then she had waited while I was on my first tour to Vietnam. In hindsight, when I take into account that we were married as teenagers, that we had three sons early in our lives, and that I had been mostly an absentee husband and father, it is clear that all the ingredients were coming together for marriage problems. I knew it was time to arrange for a better family environment, so I requested assignment to the 10th Special Forces Group, in Germany. The 10th had a somewhat easier training schedule, and I expected that the change of scenery would help our family grow together like never before. I dreamed of having our family together in Germany.

Barbara and the boys learned to spend time doing family activities without me. They often enjoyed picnics with other wives and children at a local park near Pope Air Force Base, just outside of Fort Bragg. There the kids played and explored while the mothers laughed and visited with one another. All too often the women ended up discussing what their husbands did for a living, and the danger they continually faced. They were all very proud of their men, but feared for their lives and also feared a dreaded day of disappointment and sorrow when they might face life alone. Whenever time permitted, I would spend time with the boys. I once bought a football and helped them learn how to throw it, and would sometimes come home and surprise them on the playground near our apartment. After getting them dizzy on the merry-go-round we would walk home, holding hands with Mike and Bobby, while Joe rode piggy-back. Mike was a quiet one. It was not unusual to see him sitting in a chair pondering things and thinking much too deeply for a boy his age. His serious nature made him consider things that most kids his age didn't even dream of. Bobby was more of a loner and had somewhat of an independent personality. He was mechanical and always wanted to take something apart and 'fix it'. Little Joe was the clown of the family, and seemed to always be in the photographs, home movies and at center stage. His playful antics kept everybody in stitches. We lived relatively simple lives and did not over purchase. We saved money the best we could but probably over spent a bit for Christmas. Sometimes we had to get creative to find places for the kids presents, because they would not all fit under the Christmas tree. Christmas mornings were magical for all of us.

In August of 1963, I was again separated from my family and was sent to Pathfinder school in Ft. Benning, Georgia. The Army had discovered that there were combat situations that called for pinpoint placement of a few airborne troops, but without all the attention of falling parachutes. They developed a system of dropping troops from an altitude so close to the ground that there was just barely enough time for the parachute to fully deploy before hitting the ground. When troops are dropped at tree-top level, there is no time for the enemy to shoot them out of the sky. In the Pathfinder technique, the soldier stands at the door of the aircraft and waits as the plane dives toward the drop zone. As the plane begins to climb out of the dive, the soldier drops away, with the parachute rapidly deploying. This results in a ride that is unmatched at any amusement park. If there is a problem with your parachute, there is no time to deploy a reserve chute.

The soldier makes one wide swing, and in only a few seconds is on the ground. Following this training, I went to Jumpmaster school for learning to control large Airborne maneuvers. Upon completion of this school, I continued to have specialty training, by completing Long Range Reconnaissance Patrol (LRRP) school, SCUBA school, Underwater Demolition school, continuous hand-to-hand combat training, one school after another, month after month. We were continually on long range exercises that sometimes would take us fifty or more miles through forested areas all over the United States. We would be dropped off by helicopter or parachute drop with only a clue as to where we were and then would orient ourselves and find our way back to a base camp. We were an unusual breed of soldier and occasionally would 'cheat' our way home. On one mission we were given several days to get back to our base camp, but after coming to a highway, we decided to hitch hike most of the way back. We found a hotel not far from camp and enjoyed a three day vacation before donning our gear and walking the few miles back to base camp.

Endless training, one class after another, yet always I would check on my request for the assignment in Germany. Between the different specialty schools, I was sent to several military hospitals in order to continue my surgical training. I was continually exposed to more clinical and surgical procedures, and I felt confident that I could perform any medical procedure that I may be called upon to perform. In November of 1963, while on a training exercise, I learned of the death of President John F. Kennedy. I was deeply saddened, and felt I had lost a true friend. It had been two years since he personally awarded me the Green Beret, yet it seemed like it had happened only a few weeks earlier.

On several training exercises we were taken by submarine off the coast of North Carolina where we were deployed, underwater, for mock missions. Underwater deployments are not for the claustrophobic. I performed several of them, and of the things I have no desire to repeat, climbing out of a submerged submarine is somewhere near the top of the list. In January of 1964, I was sent to Ft. Wolters, Texas, for helicopter flight training. Barbara and the boys moved to nearby Mineral Wells, where we rented a nice house while I spent the next six months in flight school. I was gone long hours, but because I was home more often, things were better in our marriage. Because I knew that my unit, the 5th Special Forces Group, would eventually get another Vietnam assignment, I continually tried for the 10th Group assignment in Germany. I was sure that going back to Vietnam would surely finish my marriage. In June I was sent back to Ft. Bragg for more reconnaissance training. Barbara had not seen her family for some time, so I drove her and the kids back to Montana and left them there while I returned to Ft. Bragg where I began my most favorite training of all---Ranger School. This consisted of two months of some of the most physically exhausting training available. The reason I enjoyed it so much was that I had already been through everything they had to throw at me. Ranger School was merely a review for those of us who were A-Team qualified. In addition, it served to give us more confidence in ourselves, simply because we were able to smile at things that caused some of the class members to wash out. Early the first morning of training, they ran us for several miles, then marched us into a river up to our shoulders. Once in the middle of the river, we were forced to stand at attention until the commanding officer would arrive and welcome us to Ranger School. We had not as yet eaten breakfast, but stood there at attention for four hours before the Sergeant in charge drove up on the bridge. Climbing out of his jeep, the Sergeant informed us that the Captain had been delayed, but would soon arrive to welcome us. I knew exactly what the training staff was trying to do. The whole idea of the first day was to weed out the ones who were not mentally and emotionally fit for Ranger school. Any man there could have marched out of the river and ran for twenty miles, but a third of them could not stand at attention in a river, all day, and just wait. Several more hours passed, and finally came the moment we had been waiting for. After eight hours of standing at attention, in water up to our necks, waiting for the Captain to welcome us to Ranger school, he drove onto the bridge, and said quite simply, "Welcome to Ranger School", then he drove away. The Sergeant in charge then marched us out of the river and onto the road, and ran us for ten miles. By the time the sun was down, we were cleaning up and getting ready for our first meal of the day. Several of the soldiers got sick of what they thought was harassment with this maneuver, and quit Ranger School the first day. On another day, we marched all day long, without food. Those in charge kept telling us that we would have a nice chicken dinner back at the field camp. When we finally returned to camp, long past dark, we stood in line as they handed each of us a live chicken from the back of a truck. I nearly split in two with laughter, at the sight of all those starving and disappointed men walking around with live chickens and no cooking facilities. Eventually we all were able to cook the chickens over open fires and have our long awaited chicken dinners. I loved Ranger School, and still relish the experience. I next attended Computed Air Release Parachute school, or CARP. This was a training program focused on nighttime jumps where the time and location of the jump was determined by calculations rather than by visual observation. If done correctly, you landed somewhere near where you should have. If it was done wrong, you might be ten or more miles from where you planned to land.

By September of 1964, I hadn't seen Barbara and the kids for several months. We were growing apart, and while they were with Barbara's family in Anaconda, Montana, I desperately tried to get the Germany assignment so we could have a fresh start. I was feeling lonely and frightened just at the thought of losing my family. Barbara adds: "While the boys and I loved seeing my family, and enjoying the beautiful Montana summer, still we desperately missed being with Bob. The boys needed a father as much as I needed a husband, but somehow we were unable to have either." In October, I learned that new orders were coming for my new assignment. I was excited to get the new orders because I was sure that I could call Barbara and have her pack for Germany. Finally, I thought, a new life for our family. When I actually received my orders, however, I was bitterly disappointed to learn that I would *not* be going to Germany, after all. Instead, I was being assigned to a new unit within the 5th Special Forces Group. The orders were for Detachment B-52. I learned that this new unit, called Project Delta, was being formed for special missions. The Project Delta Recon team to which I was assigned consisted of twenty-five combat experienced, reconnaissance specialists chosen from qualified A-Teams. These men were hand-picked for a unit which would be used for especially sensitive missions. Project Delta was to be the epitome of guerilla warfare and over the next year would make a name for itself that would strike fear in the hearts of the enemy. I did *not* want this assignment. I wanted only to take my family to Germany and try to mend my troubled marriage. I had my orders, though, and there was little I could do about it. Project Delta team training began, and continued over the next several months. But, because I was always gone on training exercises, it didn't make sense to bring Barbara and the kids back to Ft. Bragg from Montana. I felt my grip on our family slipping away, and it was as if the very doors of life were closing on me. Training continued day and night, and though my heart was empty, I simply had no choice but to continue with full effort and dedication to our team. Project Delta had three missions: First, Pilot Rescue. The United States was becoming heavily involved in Vietnam, and we were continually losing pilots. By this time there had been many fighter aircraft shot down over Vietnam, and many pilots had become prisoners of war. One of our missions would be to establish a network of locations from which downed pilots could be rescued, and then to rescue them. Second, Reconnaissance. This was suspected to be the majority of our work. We would carefully slip into enemy territory, determine their strengths, and then return and report. All of us frequently radioed our reports while under enemy fire, most of my friends never returned. In theory, we would be inserted into enemy territory but never actually make contact, however of the dozens of such missions I was sent on with Delta, nearly all resulted in blood and bullets. Third, Bomb Damage Assessment. There was a great deal of enemy supply-trail bombing. One of our missions would be to assess this bombing effectiveness, then make recommendations for further bombing. The training for this area, as well as the others, continued to intensify. We became close friends and though we were very disciplined and hardened, we usually referred to one another by nicknames or last names. All the guys called me Bobby.

During the summer of 1965, the Dominican Republic was faced with a Communist uprising. There were Soviet and Cuban-trained rebels creating a serious rebellion among the populations in the outlying areas. The 82nd Airborne had been sent in to help, but they had been there for several months, and had not been able to quell the insurrection. The Special Forces were called upon to come up with a plan of their own, and several A-Teams were chosen from the 5th Group. I was called on for an unusual mission. Staff Sergeant Bob Owens, who spoke fluent Spanish, was assigned to accompany me. As medically trained soldiers, we were to dress in civilian clothes, carry no weapons, and appear more like Peace Corps volunteers than Special Operations Commandos. Before long, we were air lifted by military transport to Santa Domingo, and began our covert assignment. We were given access to all the medical supplies and Dominican Republic money that we needed, and we went from village to village offering aid and throwing great parties. Actually, we had much more fun than we were supposed to have. After only a week, we were the local heroes. Sick people were healed, new shoes were purchased, and everyone ate plenty of food at our feasts. When we felt that we had established a good relationship with the Dominicans, we began to ask simple questions about the Communist uprising. Slowly we learned everything we needed to learn about where the rebels were located, when they were on patrols, and just who they were. As we gained the information, we sent radio messages to the A-Teams staged in the area. These teams intercepted the rebels, and after a few dozen firefights, the rebellion was over. We had extinguished the uprising in less than six weeks, and at last were on our way home. Without doubt, this was the easiest and most enjoyable assignment of my military career. During our time with the villagers, we found one man who wanted American money for sharing the information he had about the rebels. We called back to headquarters and asked if they could arrange to give this man $100 in American currency. Headquarters approved the payment, and we had the money within 24 hours. After thinking about how easy that was, Owens and I smiled at each other. It was *too* easy. We called back and asked for another $200 and we got it right away. More smiles. Another call and another $1,000 was sent to us. This was too good to be true. By the time the rebellion was over and we were on our way home, we each had around $4,000 tucked away in our pants, boots, pockets, duffle bags and everywhere else. To a poor soldier, that was over a year's salary. We thought of the cars we would buy, the vacations we would go on, and the gifts we could purchase for our families. At our debriefing prior to leaving the island, the Lieutenant Colonel responsible for our mission told us that we had gained more information, and had done more to stop the rebellion, than all the other American forces combined. He praised and commended us at some length, then smiled and asked that we hand over the American money. *Rats*, we thought. They had figured out our scheme, but had continued to send us money in order to avoid ruining our morale. So, we dug through all of our gear and returned the money, then sheepishly boarded our plane and returned to the United States. We laughed about it all the way home, despite our disappointment over the lost cars and vacations. Though we were laughing on the outside we were somber on the inside, and felt lucky to have not been officially reprimanded. However, we had been through years of covert style training, so we had learned to plan for every conceivable outcome to a mission. When we got off the plane we smiled at each other, patted each other's backs, then took off our boots and removed $100 bills from our socks.

On September 22, 1965, I left Ft. Bragg with orders to join the 5th Special Forces Group, in Vietnam. I was allowed 15 days leave, so I immediately went to Anaconda, Montana, to spend time with Barbara and the boys. We had not been together for almost 10 months, and our marriage had nearly disintegrated. I wanted to be happy, and to have a wonderful vacation; and I wanted so badly to say some magic words and make our family happy again. Reality can be bitter, however, because I truly didn't believe I would ever see them again. I tried to absorb as much of the family vision as I could so that I could later recall the memories of their voices, their clothing, their laughter and the warmth of their hugs. While there, Barbara put on as good of a front as possible, and organized a party to celebrate my 27th birthday. Though I was surrounded with the family that I loved, I was dreadfully lonely within. At that time, Mike's third grade teacher sent a letter home and asked that I come to their school in military dress and Green Beret to speak on the subject of patriotism. The next day I visited Washington Elementary school in Anaconda, Montana and in doing so, I felt well received by them all. More importantly, I felt loved and admired by Mike. Several days later, after doing all I could to enjoy the moment, I said goodbye to Barbara and our sons, then flew westward into what would become the most difficult year of my life. As we hugged and bid farewell to one another, the tears were too difficult to hold back. The boys cried desperately and Barbara fell to her knees to comfort them as I forced myself to turn and walk away. My last view of them was a sorrowful scene that made me question my life's purpose. The people I loved most of all were huddled together and sobbing, wishing I could stay home, but knowing I had to go. My own tears flowed freely, as I did not expect to ever see them again. I remember wishing I still worked on the railroad, and recalled the days, only ten years earlier, when I walked to work every day and returned home in the evening. I remembered taking little Mike out to see my old car and walking with him in my arms through the backyard. I thought of the playground near our home in Fort Bragg where I played with the boys, and remembered the happiness we enjoyed on our Blue Ridge Mountain camping trip after my first trip to Vietnam. Now, life was altogether different. I dared not hope that there would be another wonderful experience when, or if, I returned. The sobs of my loved ones still haunting my ears, and the memory of Barbara crying and hugging the children, all of them sobbing on their knees, would stay with me during the long trip to the bloody shores of Vietnam.

Dear Daddy,

It was sad to see you leave again for the war.   Mama said you are in the hospital because you got hurt real bad.   Did you get shot? I know you will be okay and I know you will come home. Last time you went to the war I asked God to save you and I just know that He will keep his promise He made to me Last night, me and Bobby and Joey were sitting on the couch with Mama and she started to cry. Then me and Bobby started to cry and then Joey did too. We didn't say anything, we just cried. It is almost Christmas and we miss you.   I remember when you came to the school with me to talk to my class. All the kids believe me now, when I tell them you are a real Green Beret. I think the neatest thing that ever happened to me is when you walked down the school hall holding my hand and wearing your uniform and shiny boots and medals and the Green Beret. I will never forget about that.   I am in cub scouts now and have a blue cub scout shirt. School is okay and I like my teacher. I can't wait until you come home.

Love,
Mike

CHAPTER SIX
Plei Me

Our C-141 touched down in Saigon on the morning of October 9, 1965. The rest of the Delta members had arrived some time before me. I was delayed getting there due to the Dominican Republic mission.   It was hot and humid when I arrived and I recognized the sights, sounds and smells from my first tour there. When I got off the plane, someone informed me that the Special Forces Reporting Station was at the other end of the runway, about a mile away, and there was no bus, no jeep, and no one to help with my gear. That was

typical. Project Delta philosophy was that you could find
your own way, find your own food, and find your own bed.
Consequently, I carried my gear to the reporting station and
asked for a flight to Nha Trang. The Special Forces officers
had spent months choosing the twenty-five men for the
Project Delta recon teams. They chose us from among the
combat experienced Special Forces units around the world.
They had gone to a lot of trouble to get this unit together.
Though we felt honored to have been selected, we were
subdued by the danger we knew awaited us. When I arrived
in Nha Trang, I received my government issue of weapons and
supplies. I was given an M-16, an Army .45 caliber pistol,
and a .25 caliber fully automatic pistol. I had only been in
Vietnam for four or five hours when I finally walked into the
small Headquarters of Detachment B-52. I was greeted by
Major Charles Beckwith. He stood taller than most, weighed
well over 200 pounds, and looked more like an NFL
linebacker than a military officer. He was always half-shaven,
knew more cuss words than any ten men, and was just plain
rough. His first words to me were, "Good to meet you,
Bobby. If I don't get you killed over here, it won't be my
fault...'cause I'm putting you right in the middle of 'em".
Rats, I thought. Major Beckwith told me to get with Sergeant
Gifford because he needed another team member for an
immediate mission. I walked down the lane, found Gifford,
and in half an hour we were in a chopper looking for a landing
zone where we would spend the night. I had been in the
country for eight hours but had not been offered a meal. That
was also typical. In Delta you found your own meals. An
hour or so later, when we landed back at base camp, we got
supplies to last five days. I grabbed a quick bite to eat. By

nightfall on my first day in the country we had landed in a rainy jungle in the Central Highlands and were looking for bad guys. An enemy battalion had been expected to move through this area, and it was our mission to study them and determine their strengths. After three days of reconnaissance, we found no sign of enemy units, and were airlifted out. The date was October 12. During those first few days on patrol with Gifford, I had plenty of time to ask about Major Beckwith. He had recently replaced Major Black who had been killed. Gifford told me that Beckwith was a little crazy, but that he was extremely loyal to his men, and would stand beside us under any circumstances. He said that Beckwith would even go to the pub and buy you a drink now and then. Still, these words of comfort didn't make me feel any better about his warning that he would get me killed. When we returned to the camp, I was dirty, tired and hungry. It would feel good to get a real meal and sleep in a real bed. On my way to do so, Beckwith stopped me and cheerfully asked, "Hey, Bobby, wanna go to Plei Me?" I didn't know where Plei Me was, but I thought he wanted to buy me a drink, so I said that I would be glad to go with him. "Good, good..." he growled, "Come on." So I went down to the airfield with Beckwith, looking for the beer hall. But there *was* no beer hall. Instead there were dozens of aircraft and hundreds of troops preparing for a mission. I asked Beckwith what was going on and discovered that Plei Me was not a beer joint, but a military camp that was under siege by the North Vietnamese. Americans were in the camp, along with hundreds of South Vietnamese troops, and the forces in the camp were about to be over-run by the enemy. A few days earlier, a battalion from an armored division had started to fight their way in from the outside, but had not been able to get through to help the surrounded camp. The Special Forces were called on to lead a company in from another side. I wondered how we were going to survive fighting through the encirclement when an armored battalion couldn't even do it, but it didn't matter. In a few more minutes we were on our way to Pleiku, the staging area for our mission. Once in Pleiku, Major Beckwith laid out the strategy to get us into the besieged camp. Over three hundred men would be airlifted in UH-1 Huey choppers to an area about seven miles from Plei Me. We would land in six waves, the first wave consisting of smaller patrols who would clear the landing zone of enemy. One of the first patrols would have the responsibility of being the *point team*. That would be the team that leads the way through the enemy encirclement. I had hoped like heck that I would be on the last wave, but Beckwith looked at me and said, "Bobby, I want you to take the point team". I tried not to show my disappointment.

The plan was for us to fly in at daybreak, then make our way in to Plei Me by sundown. This was an unusual assignment for Delta. We were on a mission with hundreds of Vietnamese Rangers who, until this very day, were strangers. I was assigned eight South Vietnamese Rangers to use on my Point Team. Eight total strangers. I spoke some Vietnamese, but none of these men understood English. It was almost dark by this time, and we were scheduled to leave just before daylight. That gave me only a few hours to give them some training and instruction on how we would proceed. I did as well as I could, then spent my fourth restless night in the country, under a tree. As daylight arrived, my point team flew into the landing zone, and cleared the area for the next wave. I had the ominous responsibility of making the decision to abort the whole mission if there were any serious problems. I was happy to find that there was no enemy in the vicinity, but disturbed to discover that we had been dropped off five miles short of the landing zone. I decided not to abort, but quickly searched my maps for a new route into Plei Me. When Beckwith landed, he found me and asked for my assessment of the situation. I was downright angry about getting dropped at the wrong LZ, and pointing to the map, I snapped, "We're not here, we're *here!* And we're not going in this way, we're going in *this* way." Beckwith liked that approach, and slapped me on the back, saying, "Go get 'em, Bobby!" I set up my point team and began the patrol. A half hour later, we ran into an enemy patrol. Bullets began flying towards us but even with the confusion of the gunfire, my new squad of Vietnamese Rangers handled themselves well. I directed our counterattack towards the ambush and the enemy quickly retreated. During the short exchange of gunfire, my point man was killed. Within seconds the next man had moved into the point position and we continued our movement. There were three hundred men coming along behind us, and I could not stop my team just because somebody was shooting at us. If I thought that an enemy force in front of me was significant, I could call for a platoon to move in for an assault on the force, but to stop our progress because of one man killed would have been exactly what the enemy wanted. We knew full well that we would make contact with the enemy, and that they would fire on us. We knew that before we landed. We also knew the point man had little or no chance of surviving the day. The point man knew that as well as we did. It was brutal, but that was the way it had to be. With the second man in point position, we continued our movement and after marching a mile deeper into the enemy territory, we encountered another enemy position. They opened fire on us and the new point man was killed, along with two other men on my right flank. Four now dead. The enemy gunfire was much heavier this time, and I knew this was a larger enemy force which our point team, or what was left of it, could not defeat. I reported back to Beckwith that we were being fired on by at least two heavy machine guns and other light weapons, and then called for one platoon to move to my right and engage the enemy. The fighting lasted about twenty minutes, after which we continued the patrol with a fifth man in the point position. I knew how the remaining men on my team felt. We had little chance of surviving the next few hours, and we were a little edgy. The last four men in the lead had been killed in their tracks. It should not be difficult to imagine how much more caution each new point man exercised. We were all more nervous, more watchful, and moved forward with more care. Even so, within an hour we were engaged by a much larger force than the last two. We spared no ammunition against that enemy force, but their firepower was intense and the four remaining men on my point team were killed. I called for two platoons to move forward and engage this new enemy force. An intense firefight ensued and lasted for over two hours. A lot of good men, on both sides, died during those two bitter and bloody hours. When the fighting was over, Beckwith came forward and we discussed the situation. We had been delayed by the several firefights and by the additional five miles we had to cover. I told Beckwith that it was not likely that we could fight our way in before dark. He decided to spend the night where we were, then continue on in the morning. Beckwith asked me if I wanted another eight men for my point team. There was no way I could properly instruct a team in the night jungle with the enemy all around us, so I told Beckwith I would have to be the next point man, myself. He said he would be right behind me and back me up, but I was not anxious to have the position of point man. The life expectancy of the eight men on my team had been about an hour. I walked back into the middle of the three hundred Rangers, and spent another restless night. Though surviving my full year in Vietnam was not likely, by the fifth night in the country I wondered if I would even survive the first week. The following day we traveled all the way to the main road into Plei Me and then to within six hundred yards of the main gate, all without enemy contact. It seemed strange to me that we didn't run into any more enemy while I was the point man. They knew we were coming, and should have been waiting for us. I was somewhat more cautious as we neared the main road. It was only logical that the enemy would have the road well protected, so we approached carefully. I did not know there were news reporters with us, but they had been on the sixth wave of troops to land. As we reached the road, two of the reporters moved closer onto the road in order to take some photographs. All at once the main body of our force was fired on by several machine gun locations. One reporter was killed instantly. Another, by the name of Flynn, who later told us he was the son of the actor Errol Flynn, had his right eye torn out by a bullet. He survived, but others of our men were killed on that road. I searched for the machine gun locations, threw two grenades, and helped direct our firepower into the enemy locations while our main force continued toward the camp. We killed most of the enemy involved in the ambush and continued fighting as we moved toward the main gate. The dead and dying were strewn along the road, crying and moaning. I was embarrassed to see our force get a little out of order as we ran down the road with some of the troops in a bit of a panic. We gathered the wounded and the dead, and within another hour we were all inside the camp.

The situation in Plei Me was much more desperate than we had anticipated. There were stacks of dead men at the front gate. We were all sickened by the smell of over a hundred bodies that had been lying, for days, in the heat of the sun. Before the siege was lifted, there would be many more dead men in those stacks. We discovered that an enemy battalion of over a thousand men had moved into position, and was poised for an attack. Even with the air support we were getting, it was clear to all of us that our small force could not repel a full attack by the enemy without sustaining very heavy casualties. Mortar rounds had been falling day and night for weeks, and continued to explode in camp, killing and maiming, while we were there. We were still hoping for arrival of the armored battalion that had started into Plei Me four days before us, but which was still trying to get through the enemy encirclement. Beckwith took command of the camp. After assessing the situation, he decided that the first thing we should do was prepare an escape route in the event we needed to use it. There was a large clear area on one side of the triangular camp and it seemed that the enemy fire was coming mostly from the other side of camp. Beckwith ordered two Ranger companies to make a wide sweep of the clear area to drive out the enemy, and allow for our possible escape route. While the two platoons were made up of South Vietnamese soldiers, he also asked for me and an American Special Forces advisor named Captain Pusser, to accompany the patrol. We left the relative safety of the camp and began moving across the empty field. I was patrolling near Captain Pusser as we got about halfway through the field. Suddenly a hidden enemy machine gun at the edge of the clearing began firing at us. Our men were being shot and were dropping all around me and the less disciplined South Vietnamese soldiers began retreating. I fell to the ground, searching for the machine gun location and thought that if I was careful I could get all the way to the enemy machine gun without being killed. Captain Pusser, who had been near me when the shooting started, was killed instantly by a shot in the forehead. Everyone was in retreat, with the dead and dying laying all over the field. Though I wanted to retreat back to the camp with the rest of them, I still felt that I could get to the machine gun location. I began moving toward the enemy, circling to their right and avoiding bullets. Miraculously, I made it all the way there without being shot. I was able to move close enough to the machine gun to empty my M-16 rounds into the enemy position. I wanted to reload immediately and be ready to fire again, so I rolled onto my left side to grab another ammunition clip. Just as I rolled over, I felt the sting of an enemy bullet in my right hip. I looked up and immediately saw a sniper in a tree directly in front of me, and two other snipers in separate trees just beyond the machine gun location. The sniper who had shot me was taking aim again, just as I discovered him. He probably had my head in his sights and only missed killing me because I rolled over to reload just as he fired. Knowing that they were deadly accurate, I rolled over one full turn then quickly killed that sniper, and then the other two. Captain Pusser had probably been killed by one of these snipers. When the guns were all quiet, I turned to witness the scene of death spread before me. Why was I spared? The dead and the dying were scattered around the field the way twigs lay under an old tree. Now that the fighting was over, the day seemed like any other day except for the blood and sorrow lying before me, the silence of the countryside being broken by the moans of the dying. It was all so odd. I went back to the body of Captain Pusser and, carrying his body, I limped back to the camp trying to conceal myself while distant enemy soldiers fired a few rounds toward me. Beckwith had been watching my assault on the machine gun location, and when I returned he hugged me fiercely and kissed my cheek. He nominated me for awards and medals, and called me a hero, but I didn't feel upbeat about any of it. I was tired, sweaty, bloody and sombered by the death I had both witnessed . . . and caused. A doctor at the camp removed the bullet in my hip and finding no bone damage, he simply stitched me up. Then, while a platoon was sent out to retrieve the wounded and the bodies from the field, I found a C-ration meal and ate it under the protection of a sheet of metal that was leaned against a short wall. The moans of the wounded, the smell of the dead and the explosions of mortars were my only dinner companions. I thought of Barbara and the boys.

We fought the enemy from our camp at Plei Me for another two nights and three days. On the second day of the siege, we got an unusual radio call. President Johnson was patched through via radio and spoke with Beckwith directly to discuss the situation in the camp and to assure us that he supported us and wished us all the best. The North Vietnamese had mortar and machine gun locations that overlooked the camp, and were causing terrible damage to our forces. Occasionally an enemy platoon would stage an assault, but would usually be repelled before breaking into our camp. As I fought from a machine gun location in the center of the front line, their assaults would scare the gee-whizzlies out of me. Hundreds of enemy soldiers screaming towards us would raise the hair on any man's neck. During one of these attacks, enemy soldiers fought their way right up to the camp fences and through our lines about a hundred yards to my right. There was hand to hand combat as enemy soldiers began making their way into the camp and it looked as if we might be over run. We were outnumbered three to one and the situation became increasingly desperate. It was during this battle that the 'Flaming Arrow' signal was given to the Air Force. Flaming Arrow was a code phrase that called for top priority of any Air Force fighters in the vicinity to immediately come to the rescue. Several F-105 Thunderchief pilots, en route to another mission, were given a change of orders to fly directly to Plei Me. Beckwith had radio contact with the pilots as they neared the camp and told them where to lay their firepower. Without being there, personally, you cannot imagine the awesome firepower of one of these combat aircraft. The pilots knew that enemy soldiers were within the camp and that the situation was desperate with hand to hand fighting. They flew dangerously close to the enemy fire, at great risk to themselves, in order to place their firepower on the enemy and not injure our own people. Napalm, bombs and 20mm cannon stopped the enemy from completely overpowering the camp. Eventually the attack subsided and we were left to care for the dead and wounded. The only thing that kept me sane at this time was a letter from Barbara and the boys that I had in my pocket. Barbara made every effort to pick my spirits up, and always expressed her love and support, but I knew that in all likelihood our marriage would never again see a happy day. I did appreciate her thoughts, however, and the letters they wrote. One afternoon, a tough old Sergeant by the name of Lafoya, and myself, were assigned the task of assaulting the machine gun location that was causing the most serious damage to our location. Our objective was to get close enough to use a flame-thrower. After scrambling through enemy bullets for about a hundred yards, we were unhappy to have trouble lighting the flame thrower. Today I can laugh about the darn flame-thrower, but on that day I was terrified with the bullets and enemy forces buzzing around us as we desperately tried, but failed, to light the flame. We returned through the machine gun fire to a relatively safe spot, regrouped our thoughts, and decided to accomplish our objective the old-fashioned way. Sergeant Lafoya and I, covered by three South Vietnamese Ranger platoons, made another trip to the machine gun nest. Lafoya got within twenty feet of the enemy machine-gunners and killed them with a grenade. Dozens of men had been killed by that single machine gun site. On the last night of the siege, the North Vietnamese sent a five-hundred man force at us. Hundreds and hundreds of enemy soldiers could be seen running through the grass toward us. The bullets, explosions, cries and terror of night fighting do not fade from a person's memory. Even these many years later, the scenes of Plei Me are vivid in my mind. Even now, the picture of hundreds of enemy soldiers racing towards us, illuminated by flares, and with their rifle muzzles flashing, and the continuous sound of gunfire, and with bullets snapping and thudding all around, and the flash and thunder of mortars, and with smoke drifting away as if it didn't care about the haunting scene, and with the dark stains of blood on my comrades, and the crying of a few women and children in the camp, and with the mud on our clothes, hands and boots, and with the fiercest determination in each of us to fight and win, all this has never left my memory. Gradually, with each failed effort to over-run our camp, their resolve seemed to weaken. We were continually re-supplied with weapons, ammunition and food while the enemy was repeatedly beat back. Their final assault of a couple of hundred men racing toward us was a weak effort. We had killed hundreds of them in the few days of fighting. By this time, we knew there was little chance we would be overrun. That was when the armored division finally made it to Plei Me. The next day we were airlifted out, and I was finally able to spend a night, my ninth night in Vietnam, in a regular cot. I never did go to a hospital for my hip wound. The bullet had not damaged the bone and the doctor in the camp had cleaned the wound well and stitched it tight. It seemed silly to go to a hospital now, after I had been walking around and fighting for the last few days. The injury was sore and stiff, but was otherwise healing fine. Besides, it was time for my next mission.

CHAPTER SEVEN
Nightmares

I spent three restful days at Special Forces Headquarters in Nha Trang. My hip was healing well, and I was ready for my next assignment. The enemy force that attacked Plei Me was part of a much larger force. They were now retreating the way they had come, along a branch of the Ho Chi Minh Trail which is just outside the borders of Vietnam, in Cambodia. A reconnaissance mission was ordered to determine the strength, capabilities and escape route of this enemy. Sixteen Delta men, four 4-man teams, flew to our Pleiku staging area where we were given a Tactical Area of Responsibility (TAR). One team was assigned an area inside Cambodia and the others were assigned an area just inside the Vietnam border. Each team would spend three to five days patrolling a strip of ground approximately 10 miles long. On October 24, 1966, we boarded the choppers and began the mission.

My team was sent into Cambodia. We understood this to be especially sensitive, politically, so the intent was to be extremely cautious and never make any contact with the enemy or with Cambodian civilians. The military would call it a mistake if we happened to be discovered. The enemy forces were using a branch of the Ho Chi Minh trail and it was important to observe them and learn about them. We did not plan to shoot anybody. Our area of responsibility included a strip of ground five miles wide and 24 miles long, and perpendicular to the Vietnam border. We were dropped off 24 miles into Cambodia and slowly made our way Eastward toward Vietnam. On the second day of travel, we crossed a branch of the Ho Chi Minh and got a first-hand look at the supply movement. We had made good time travelling and then decided we could spend some extra time gathering information about troops and supplies that would be valuable to the intelligence people back at headquarters. We stayed a couple hundred yards off the trail, and moved north one full day, traveling slowly to avoid mines and booby traps. There was some enemy movement, but we had time to go right onto the road to take measurements and gather valuable first-hand information about this infamous trail. By nightfall, we began moving toward Vietnam. The next afternoon we heard Air Force jet strikes and figured one of the other teams was in trouble and had called for air support. We continued our eastward travel, and the next morning made radio contact with our air command. They gave us a position fix, and directed us to a location where we were picked up a few hours later.

My last few days in October, Barbara's 26th birthday, were spent on a recon mission in an area North of Pleiku. A firefight with the enemy resulted in another minor bullet wound to my lower right leg. The last two sentences do not begin to describe the details and specifics of the mission, nor do any of the stories in this book fully describe all the events completely. That level of detail is not critical to this biography, because the book is not intended to achieve any more than to offer the reader a glimpse of the reality of war. Upon returning from this particular mission, I had a short hospital stay and then a few more days of rest. Letters from Barbara and the boys began arriving shortly thereafter. Barbara had heard reports about the difficulties at Plei Me from some of the other wives, still in Fort Bragg. They had sent newspaper articles to her that mentioned my name as having been decorated for my efforts at Plei Me. Naturally, she was worried about what had happened, and wrote to ask for some details. Reading letters from the family helped erase the vision of them huddled together, crying, as I left them.

In the first week of November, George Hoagland and I were sent on a recon mission in an area North of Bien Hoa (Ben Wah), known as the Black Forest. We were assigned four Vietnamese Rangers. Our H-34 helicopter was piloted by a man named Khoi Boi, a Vietnamese officer we called 'Cowboy'. He was a particularly skilled pilot, and would fly into any amount of danger. He kept his head, never panicked, and always seemed to be grinning. Some of the guys had bought him a cowboy hat and a six-shooter pistol to wear on his belt. Cowboy became somewhat of a folk hero and was well known among Delta people, as well as other Special Forces groups. He was respected by all of us in Delta, and we considered it our good fortune whenever he was the pilot of one of our missions. As Cowboy piloted us into our landing zone, we were hit by a barrage of small-arms fire. The chopper began smoking, the motor died, and we were on our way down for a crash landing. Cowboy performed a perfect auto-rotation, despite being only a few hundred feet high when we lost power. We hit the ground hard, and the rotor blades bent down, shearing off into the ground upon impact. I quickly organized the team and saw Cowboy climb down from the cockpit with that big grin on his face. He stood back and smiled at the chopper, broken blades and smoking motor, as if he were an artist admiring his work. There were no tracers on the enemy gun-fire that had shot us down, so we didn't know for sure where the enemy might be. I rigged the chopper for demolition, and prepared for escape and evasion. In theory, we were never supposed to be seen by the enemy, and would never make contact with them. The theory usually did not work so well, as we nearly always ended up in a firefight. We were actually spies, and whenever we got shot at, our secrecy was compromised, so the mission was cut short. We could not very well do our reconnaissance mission if the bad guys knew we were there. However, looking at the positive side of things, when they were shooting at us, we could tell how many of them were shooting, we could often see their clothing and then knew what type of enemy force they were, and hearing the gun shots, we could tell what kind of weapons were making holes in us. So, even when the mission was compromised, there was still intelligence gathered. After making radio contact with our command chopper we were given directions to a pick-up zone. We destroyed the chopper and we moved cautiously toward our pick-up location. By dark we were back at camp. I reported the mission to Beckwith exactly as it happened, and he simply growled, "Good, good . . . try not to get shot down tomorrow night!" I hoped he was joking, but I knew better. He had told me he would probably get me killed, and had spent the last month sending me right into the middle of 'em, just as he promised. The following morning we received orders to execute the same mission with the same team and in the same place. We landed, without incident, not more than a thousand feet from where we had been shot down the night before. Cowboy was only on the ground for a few seconds as we unloaded. I turned and caught a glimpse of him as he flew home for his next assignment. That was the last time I saw Cowboy. A few weeks later, he was killed when his chopper was shot down on a mission to pick up some wounded men. I moved the team quickly to a location where we would spend the night before beginning our patrol. The jungle was not very dense in this area, and there were a lot of wild boar and peacocks. When these animals heard any unusual sounds at night, they made a lot of noise and could give away our location. In areas like this, we would spend a quiet night and not move until about a half-hour after sunrise when the animals could not so easily make us known to the enemy. I had been feeling very sick and weak for several days and thought it was due to so many missions in such a short time. I decided to eat more, and would rather have perished than to have gone on sick call. In Delta we just didn't complain about little things like feeling sickly. In the morning we began our patrol. I had one Vietnamese Ranger at point, followed by me, then the rest of the team. About an hour after we started, we were hit by small-arms fire, and the point man was shot. I didn't want to leave him if he was still alive and needed help, and I needed to retrieve his equipment. So I left the team where they were, and carefully moved back to where the point man had been shot. I found him dead. I was on one knee retrieving his maps and equipment when I looked up and saw an enemy soldier standing about ten feet away. Our eyes met at the same instant and the picture of his face is burned into my memory forever. There is a switch on the side of an M-16 rifle. I always kept the switch on the 'safe' position, then moved it to 'semi-automatic' to shoot. We never used 'full automatic' fire. I had my right thumb on the switch, and without intending to do so, I moved the switch to the fully automatic position. Without hesitation, I fired first and killed him instantly. A dozen bullets hit him in a line from his belly to his head. At close range, the gunfire caused terrible damage. The horror of that moment is seared into my memory forever and my eyes will forever burn with tears because of that brutal event. I didn't sleep a full night for the next four years without revisiting that awful image. During all the intense combat experiences I faced, there was never any hesitation about my decisions. Every action was quick, decisive and automatic. The feelings of terror did not affect me until after I was asleep back at camp. I began moving back toward the rest of the team when I heard enemy gunfire behind me. At the same instant, I felt the shock of a grenade and the stinging spray of shrapnel across my back. As I hurried to my team, blood ran down my back and bloodied my pants down to my knees. Hoagland had already made radio contact to report our situation, and requested a pick-up. We moved to the designated location and were successfully airlifted back to camp. I had been feeling sick for days with sweats and a high fever. When I reported to Beckwith, he recognized the symptoms of malaria. Several other Delta team members had already been diagnosed with it and we were going to be transferred to a hospital at Camp Zama, in Japan, for treatment. I had been in Vietnam for about forty days, most of it in the jungle. I had been wounded twice, shot down once, and had malaria. I was glad for a hospital stay. There were four Delta soldiers from Camp Zama who had malaria. The other three were close friends of mine, and we became even closer during the next five weeks at the hospital. Bob Cavanaugh, Frank Badolati, Ron Terry and myself stayed in bed for a week or so, and then began to feel well enough to see the sights and eat at Japanese restaurants. I took a few days longer to recuperate because the doctors discovered I had *two* types of malaria and the medication took longer to adjust. In January of 1966, the others were sent back to Nha Trang, but I was held back for an extra two weeks. I spent that time reliving some of the bad situations I had been in, and found myself wanting to block out some of the memories with beer. I drank a lot during those weeks. One afternoon I came back to the hospital with beer on my breath, and was discovered by a big, mean, ugly nurse who hollered at me and threatened to take my pants. That was her way of keeping me in my room. I had more to think about than losing my pants, so I ripped them off, along with everything else I was wearing, and threw them at her. I then walked naked down the hall to my room. My tolerance level was quite low, to say the least, and I couldn't wait to get back with my unit. Still, I did not arrive at Nha Trang until late in January. On the way, I began to hear reports that a Green Beret operation north of Cam Rahn Bay, in a place called Bong Son, had turned disastrous, with a number of Americans being killed. As it turned out, many of my friends, including Hoagland, Badolati, Terry, and Cook-- all members of my team--had been in an intense fight with the North Vietnamese troops. All had been killed. I would have been with them, except for the longer hospitalization. Again, I had been spared. Major Beckwith was in the command and control chopper during the conflict, and had been hit in the stomach by a .51 caliber round. It nearly killed him, but he was so darn mean that he somehow survived. Thirteen years later, Beckwith and Shumate would lead the ill-fated rescue attempt of the Americans held hostage in Iran. Seven Delta members were still lost in the jungle, and two other Delta members, Hiner and Webber, badly wounded and unable to travel, had been waiting for rescue. Their situation was desperate, and each of them were badly wounded and losing consciousness as they continued to hold off the enemy soldiers attempting to over run them. As their dead friends lay scattered around the hill, Hiner and Webber faced the true terror of war. There was nothing glorious about what they were experiencing. Hiner was bleeding from a head wound and Webber had most of his left arm blown off. They were struggling to stop their own bleeding while both of them fired their weapons as rapidly as possible. Chopper crews had tried twice to get in to pick them up, but there was a nearby hilltop with an enemy machine gun location preventing rescue efforts by air. We made a special request to an air cavalry division to send in air support to help in the rescue, but they were not willing to do so for only two wounded men. We could not risk a massive Air Force strike, because there were other Delta members out there who may not have been killed. At the time, we did not know for sure where they were or who was still alive. Enemy troops moved closer and closer to our wounded friends, killing four and severely wounding Hiner and Webber. As the enemy made their final assault, the situation became even more intense. Hiner called for the command and control chopper to use their firepower on top of his own position, and was actually wounded by that 'friendly fire', but the chopper was able to slow the assault of the enemy and buy precious time for a rescue effort. There were fifteen Delta members available to assault the machine gun hill that was causing the most damage, and knock out the gun to make a chopper rescue feasible. All fifteen of us had already been dropped off at an LZ near the base of that hill.

We spent several hours fighting our way toward the top. Thirst, fatigue, sweat, terror, blood, cries, the smell of gun smoke, sorrow, determination, shock, the snap and thud of bullets, grenade explosions, dead enemy soldiers, dead friends and desperate hope. These words are inadequate descriptions of the reality of war. Enemy soldiers were thick in the countryside, and the fighting was intense. By the time we stopped the assault on the position that Hiner and Webber held, six more Delta members had been killed. *Any of them would have died all over again to rescue Hiner and Webber.* Each time another of my friends fell in his own blood, a part of me died with them. We fought our way to the top of the hill and killed or drove off the enemy. After silencing the enemy guns, we made our way to where Hiner and Webber were waiting with very serious wounds. Because we did not want to take the chance of losing more bodies in the jungle, we carried the dead on our shoulders. As we ran through more gunfire to where Hiner and Webber were waiting, some of us carried the bodies of dear friends. One of the most sorrowful memories of my life is the lonely picture of our flight through the jungle, our dead friends on our backs, and trying to get to our wounded friends to rescue them. Our cause was noble, but the cost was severe. I cannot express the deep sense of loss I felt on that awful day. A chopper was already in the air waiting for clearance and soon landed and carried Hiner and Webber to safety. They had been wounded so badly that they were not able to stay in the military, and were subsequently discharged. In this single incident, twelve Delta members had been killed, and three others had been sent home with serious injuries. There were only six of the original Delta Project recon members left after only four months of Delta operations. We spent two more days in the jungle searching for the bodies of those that had been killed. We found Paul Tracy alive and well, but the enemy soldiers were thick, and we were finally ordered to abandon the search. To our sorrow, the bodies of Frank Badolati and Ron Terry were never recovered and still lay in the fields of Bong Son. I often recall the time we enjoyed together at the hospital in Japan and hope to greet and hug them on the other side. I lost many good friends in Vietnam, but no deaths have caused me more sorrow that the deaths of Frank Badolati, Marlin C. Cook, George A. Hoagland III, and Ronald T. Terry, killed in action on January 29, 1966 at Bong Son. On a recent visit to the Vietnam Memorial in Washington, DC, I etched the names of these men from the wall.

After Bong Son, Walter Shumate, Paul Tracy, Cavanaugh, Landrum and myself, along with two other members, were sent to Taiwan for training while new Delta recon members were recruited and the Project Delta recon teams were reorganized. We had performed over a hundred missions, gathered a great deal of intelligence, found dozens of enemy locations and supply routes, destroyed supply dumps, and had made a very good name for ourselves. By this time, Delta was a name that was respected, even by the enemy. General Westmoreland occasionally met with us, and told us that we were his most valuable and reliable source of information. Following our training, we spent a week in Taiwan, and earned Chinese jump wings. These wings were awarded to us at the Taiwanese Presidential Palace where we were treated like royalty.

There was no shortage of qualified and experienced A-Team members willing to volunteer for Delta. Within a week or so, we were again fully staffed. Good men like Charles Odorizzi, Augustino Schiariello, Leo Kelland and a dozen others quickly became close friends. We had such a great respect for one another, depending on each other for our lives, that a bond of love was quickly made. The North Vietnamese had become aware of Project Delta, and thought they had destroyed Delta at Bong Son. They even published leaflets boasting that Delta no longer existed and had these leaflets dropped in several South Vietnam locations. The leaflets infuriated us, and we were anxious to get reorganized and back in operation as soon as possible. Barbara, meanwhile, was *not* anxious for me to be back in combat. She recalls, "During this intense fighting, Bob kept most of the details from me. I know he didn't want to scare me, but I couldn't have been more frightened. Every day I wondered if it would be his last. Because I thought our marriage was basically over, I sought out employment--getting my first real job since high school. While I worried about him daily, we were definitely estranged emotionally as well as physically. I honestly held little hope of ever seeing him again. My only consolation was that we had never said mean things to each other, or shouted and demeaned one another. For me, and I'm sure for the boys, life was a hell of loneliness similar to what Bob was experiencing in Vietnam."

A short time later, Don Jones, Walter Shumate, Schiarillo, Alderman, Landrum and I were called to lead point teams into the Black Forest to recon ahead of the 1st Cavalry Division. We would go in with three lead teams, each team having two Americans and four Chinese Nungs. We had not forgotten the insulting leaflets the North Vietnamese had published about us, so before we went into the Black Forest, we made up hundreds of our own leaflets. Written in Vietnamese and Chinese, and in some very rough language, we stated that Delta was alive and well and offered gruesome threats to any person who had a different opinion. We had these leaflets passed around from Saigon to Da Nang, and carried a few dozen with us on this particular mission. As we moved through the Black Forest, we encountered numerous enemy positions. More battle scenes, more nightmarish memories. After each firefight, we placed a leaflet on each of the bodies of dozens of enemy soldiers-- with bamboo stakes to make sure they didn't blow away. Occasional bodies were suspended upside down from trees with the leaflets attached. No one on my team was wounded, and the overall operation was a tremendous success. The Black Forest, which had been a haven for North Vietnamese soldiers, had begun to be cleared of the enemy. This mission served to increase our reputation as an effective guerilla force but also got us into some trouble. On our return from this mission, General Westmoreland called Delta Recon together and gave us the worst chewing out I had ever heard. When the 1st Cavalry Division came through the forest behind us, they had encountered dozens of enemy bodies, some hung upside down, with the leaflets attached. The startling scene was reported to headquarters. Westmoreland was furious over our leaflets, and yelled at us for half an hour. When at last he finished, he shouted, "What do you have to say about it"? One of our team members, Odorizzi, stepped forward and shouted in a respectful, but Sergeant-like tone, "Sir, we are

Non-Commissioned Officers in the Special Forces and in groups of two or more we bear considerable watching." Without reply, Westmoreland complimented us on our success, thanked us, and told us not to make any more leaflets. War has a way of hardening the hearts of men, and it was no different for us. When we had a few days break between missions, we drank freely. I was still plagued by the horrible image of the man I killed at close range. The nightmares had been going on nightly for a couple of months, and the only way I knew to escape the awful image was to try washing them away with strong drink. Thoughts of Barbara and my sons were continually on my mind. The letters from home were a wonderful comfort, but somehow reminded me of the family I felt I would never see again.

Bob and Barbara Wren, November 1967

Sgt. Donald Landrum

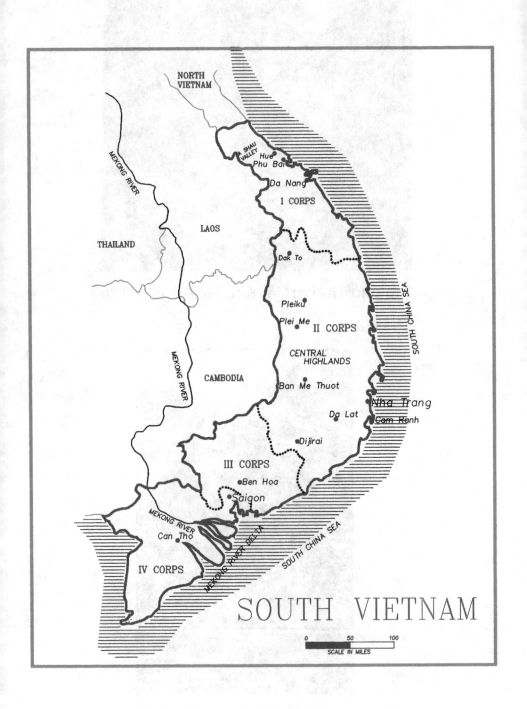

NORTH
VIETNAM

MEKONG RIVER

THAILAND

LAOS

SHAU
VALLEY
Hue
Phu Bai

Da Nang

I CORPS

Dak To

MEKONG
RIVER

Pleiku
Plei Me   II CORPS

CENTRAL
HIGHLANDS

CAMBODIA

Ban Me Thuot

Nha Trang
Da Lat
Cam Ranh

Dijirai

III CORPS

Ben Hoa
Saigon

MEKONG RIVER
Can Tho

IV CORPS

SOUTH CHINA SEA

SOUTH CHINA SEA

MEKONG RIVER DELTA

SOUTH VIETNAM

0   50   100
SCALE IN MILES

Plei Me sometime during the siege. Maj. Charles Thompson (lower rt. corner) talks to a forward air controller who is circling above the camp. A napalm strike has just been brought in on the north slope.

After the Battle of Plei Me

Back row, left to right: Capt. Baker, Lt. Berry, Capt. Hunter (camp doctor), Sgt. Moronie, SFC Robert Wren, SFC Shaw. Front row, left to right: Sgt. Loughten, Sgt. Hollaway, Major Beckwith, Major Thompson.

CHAPTER EIGHT
Five Day Run

During the last week of February, 1966, we received a report that two or three enemy battalions were massing for an invasion. The intelligence people did not know much more than that, so they called Delta for more information. Four Delta teams were sent into the area of the enemy movement, with strict orders to circle the enemy and report any information obtained. Each of the four teams had two Delta recon members with four Chinese Nungs. Landrum and I, along with four Nungs, were assigned a Tactical Area of Responsibility and supplied for a five-day mission. We flew to a thick jungle area about 150 miles South of Pleiku, into a region near the Srepok River.

When we arrived, I directed the UH-1 chopper to our previously determined landing zone, and we landed without incident. The next five days were spent moving carefully through our TAR without enemy contact. Our mission was completed as planned and we were out of food so, on the morning of our fifth day, we made radio contact and called for our airlift. As we moved toward the pick-up area, we ran into an enemy patrol. During the exchange of gunfire, my point man, a Nung, was killed. We fell back about fifty yards and heard no more gunfire. After a while, I decided to go back and retrieve the body of the point man. The other Nungs appreciated the fact that I always took the time to check on the wounded or killed point men, and retrieve the bodies of the wounded. They returned that favor with their dedication to our team. I found the point man, and as expected, he *was* dead. I was picking him up to carry his body out with us when I saw a five-man enemy patrol coming directly toward me. They were less than a hundred feet away when I rolled a grenade toward them, then crouched behind a small tree and waited for the explosion. They did not notice the grenade and continued walking toward it. I could hear their footsteps and was becoming very uneasy as they moved closer toward me. The grenade should have exploded in three to five seconds, but under these circumstances the seconds seemed more like minutes. I'm sure that I waited nearly ten seconds before I decided that the grenade had malfunctioned, and I would have to encounter them with my M-16. Just as I stood up to shoot, the grenade finally blew. At the time of the explosion, and while the rest of my body was partially covered, my face was fully exposed to the blast. The explosion was horrendous. My face burned as if it was on fire, but in spite of the blood running down my face, I was able to see and think clearly. I fired my weapon at the enemy and gratefully watched as the surviving enemy soldiers retreated. Then I lifted the body of the Nung onto my back and made my way to Landrum. My face was a terrible mess. Dozens of bits of shrapnel had smashed into my mouth and jaw area, with a larger chunk hitting me in the forehead. In addition, most of my teeth were shattered. Pieces of that shrapnel would work their way out of my gums and jaw over the next thirty years. I found Landrum and the team waiting for me when I returned, and together we continued our movement toward our pick-up zone. Landrum asked about my face, but there was neither time for talking nor first-aid. Just as we reached the pick up zone, the reinforced enemy caught up with us and began firing. I could hear our chopper coming in to get us, but I knew that the enemy fire would put the helicopter crew in danger. To place the chopper crew in that kind of danger would have been selfish and I just couldn't do it. We were tired and hungry, as well as wounded, and had completed our five-day mission. But, regardless of how badly we wanted and needed that airlift, the enemy machine gun fire was now quite heavy and I chose not to let the chopper crew face an unnecessary danger. I radioed the chopper pilot and told him to abort the pick-up. The others on the team were as disappointed as I was, but they understood the reason for the decision and fully supported me. The sounds of the rescue chopper quickly faded and we were on our own. We immediately began our escape and evasion plan--a plan that had been determined prior to the beginning of the mission. There was an A-Team camp about thirty miles to the southeast, near Ban Me Thuot. Our escape and evasion route would take us all the way to that camp unless we could find a suitable pick-up zone before we got there. I left the body of the Nung at the aborted pick-up zone. The other Nungs understood. Don Landrum was one of my best friends. He was a fierce fighter and as tough as any man I knew. I was fortunate to have him with me. By this time, the weather had begun to turn bad. Clouds were gathering, and it began to rain just as we neared the same landing zone where we had been dropped off five days earlier. The cloud cover was now too dense to call for a pick-up, so I reported my position and continued toward the A-Team camp. Just before dark, we ran into more of the enemy, and another of the Nungs was killed. This enemy unit, however, was not just a patrol. There were buckets full of bad guys, and they spared no ammunition as they fired at us. I concluded that I had unwittingly moved my team into the middle an enemy force on the march, and that we would be chased around in the middle of them until we broke out from within them. I decided that if we ran into the enemy, we should fight through them to get to the outside. I knew that in the thick of the jungle, especially in the dark, we could be concealed well enough to get through without being seen clearly enough to become a target. After all, that was how we got into the middle of them in the first place. When our point man was killed, we did not retreat, but ran toward the fire and made our way past them. We regrouped after moving through the jungle for about a hundred yards, and found that the other two Nungs had been wounded. I had my surgical kit, and treated their wounds. One of them had been shot in the side, just above the hipbone. It was a serious wound, and I had to cut away some damaged flesh to clean and suture it. The Nung did not grimace and he did not complain. Like his highly-trained comrades, he was a tough soldier.

We continued our march without rest throughout the night. We had been without food and water for most of the last day and hoped by the following morning we would find a suitable pick-up location and be airlifted out. Even so, we were disappointed by the continued clouds and rain that made a rescue helicopter landing impossible. Without stopping for more than fifteen minutes at a time, we ran all day and throughout the next night continually encountering enemy patrols that we assumed were flank guards of the main enemy force. On the morning of the third day of our run, the eighth day on the mission, we were desperately thirsty and exhausted. My badly swollen face was infected and painful, and things did not look good for any of us. The only drink available was located in a type of a hollow vine with water in it and occasional mud holes caused by the rains. We were entering our third day without food, water or sleep. We needed help as soon as we could get it, but I had not been able to make any radio contact for the last two days. On this third morning of the evasion, I decided to climb a tall tree and try the radio from up there. As luck would have it, an alert enemy soldier noticed me up in that tree, and set his gunsight on me. He fired and the shot struck me in the back. I wonder how he felt as he saw me lose my grip and fall through the branches to the ground? Somewhat dazed, I looked for blood and was relieved to discover that the radio I had been carrying on my back had absorbed the punch of the bullet. My life was spared again, but the radio was damaged and was useless. Landrum was carrying a small HT-1 radio with a very short range, but it was now our only hope to contact help when the weather cleared. We were experiencing such heavy enemy contact that I began to wonder if we really *had* broken out of the enemy encirclement. We kept gas and concussion grenades ready, and threw them every time we met the enemy. I constantly monitored our progress toward the Ban Me Thuot camp, but our progress was slow, even with 24-hour-a-day marching. On the morning of the fourth day without food or sleep, I began to think more often of Barbara and the boys. What were they doing? How would they respond if they got notice of my death? Oh, how I wished I could be with them. I wondered if I could have done things differently. I wondered if Barbara and I could still get together, and live happily ever after. I wondered if I would ever throw footballs with my sons. We continued running all that day, with frequent enemy contact, and always fighting our way through them with gas and grenades. Still cloudy and rainy. Still no radio contact. The Nung who had been wounded in the side never once murmured about his condition. I was surprised that he was still alive and with us. He had lost a lot of blood, and had been without food and rest for over four days. As we ran through the jungle my swollen chin flopped about and was as irritating as it was painful.

On the afternoon of the fifth day without food or rest, I found that we were near a small stream. I knew that the Nung would not make it much longer without plenty of water, so I gathered the canteens and cautiously made my way to the stream to fill them. By this time the weather had begun to clear, and I hoped we could make some contact with our small radio. Standard operating procedure on all Delta recon missions called for seven days of air search for teams who were missing in action. We still had two days of air search left. After filling the canteens, I heard the drone of a distant plane. A dash of hope raced through me as we attempted to contact the plane with our small radio. Fortunately, the search plane heard us. We were relieved beyond words to get a response from them. They got a fix on our location and gave us directions to a pick-up location. Landrum talked on the radio, because I could not speak clearly with my swollen face. I had ten days growth of beard that was badly infected and caked with blood. All of us were sweaty, smelly, dirty, bloody messes when the chopper crew came in to get us. We had been out for ten days and spent the last five days running, without food or sleep, bouncing off of dozens of enemy patrols. We didn't get to a hospital until we went through a complete debriefing of the information we had gathered. We reported information like the types of uniforms the enemy had, the types of weaponry they had, direction of march, amount of resistance, and so forth. We later learned that we had been in the middle of three enemy battalions that were moving through a large, broad valley toward Ban Me Thuot. The A-Team camp I was trying to reach was right in their path. The reason we spent so much time running into enemy patrols is that we were marching with the enemy, side by side, to the same place. If we had not discovered that enemy force, the A-Team camp would have been over-run by the enemy with disastrous consequences. With the information our teams had gathered, the Air Force was called in. A massive air strike wiped out the entire valley, and most of the enemy.

At the hospital, I was given some penicillin to which I had an immediate allergic reaction. My throat closed up, I was gasping for breath, and I was sure it was all over for me. After all I had been through, it seemed odd that I would die from a simple injection by an American nurse. However, a quick thinking doctor shoved an airway device down my throat and treated me for the reaction. I was spared again. The following day, General Westmoreland came to my hospital bedside, and awarded me another Silver Star and another Purple Heart. He appreciated the fact that we went through the escape and evasion difficulty rather than risk the lives of the chopper crew. There was no over abundance of pity and compassion in Delta. After a few days in the hospital, I reported back to Nha Trang Special Forces Headquarters for another mission.

CHAPTER NINE
War Is Hell

During the afternoon of March 16, Landrum and I were flying over the Ashau Valley looking for an LZ for later that evening. There had been reports of enemy activity in this area, and we had orders for a reconnaissance mission in the valley. The Ashau Valley is a very broad, flat area about thirty miles southwest of the ancient imperial capital of Hue. By this time, I was so engaged in the horrors of war that I corresponded less and less with Barbara and the boys. I felt like they were moving on in life without me, and there was absolutely nothing I could do about it. I was a good soldier, and I steeled my mind against the loneliness that was tearing my heart out, and continued to do my duty.

Though I preferred going into missions with Chinese Nungs, occasionally we were assigned Vietnamese Rangers as team members. On this mission, five Delta teams were being inserted into the valley. Walter Shumate, among my closest friends, was in the command and control chopper. From his higher altitude, he could see each of the teams being placed into their areas of responsibility. He could see my chopper fly into enemy machinegun tracers as we neared the landing zone. He watched as our chopper burst into flames and began falling to the ground, right into the enemy that had shot us down. Though certain that we couldn't have survived the crash, Shumate called for one of the choppers to fly over us for verification.

When the machine gun fire hit our helicopter, there

was an explosion, with flames rolling around the fuselage. Even so, the chopper pilot kept his head and did an excellent job of shutting off the fuel and bringing us down in auto-rotation, as far from the enemy as he could. With the chopper on fire and the enemy shooting at us, I figured the whole helicopter would explode before we had a chance to land. I felt that familiar gut-wrenching feeling as we fell helplessly to the ground. A popping sound caught my attention and I turned around to see Landrum hanging out the door shooting at the enemy. With all the confusion and in this desperate situation, here was Landrum keeping his head and fighting to the end with what we expected to be our last breaths. I was proud of him. As we hit the ground, the enemy continued to pour gunfire at us, and two of the Vietnamese Rangers began to panic. Because of the intensity of the enemy fire, I knew I couldn't call for a rescue chopper and place them in danger. The only thing on my mind was to organize another escape and evasion. I did a quick assessment of the situation and found that the helicopter radio had been damaged by gunfire and the crash landing. It was useless. Since we depended on radio contact for survival, we had a Vietnamese Ranger who was carrying a PRC-29 radio. Even under these circumstances, everything would have gone more smoothly if it had not been for a problem with the co-pilot who was literally scared stiff and frozen in his seat. This was his first mission and, even before we left camp, I noticed that he was apprehensive. The terror of being shot down in a ball of fire was more that he was prepared for. He was paralyzed with fear, and wouldn't move or respond as I tried to talk to him and pull him out of his seat. The cool-headed pilot was not injured, and was helping me with the co-pilot while Landrum and two of the Vietnamese Rangers were defending our position against the enemy. Landrum was amazing as he coordinated a fierce defensive stand with two of the Vietnamese Rangers. The two other Vietnamese soldiers were in a panic, and began to run. One of them had our radio and the other one had our maps. We all depended on those things for our survival during an escape and evasion attempt, with the radio being especially critical to us. I was still trying to get the co-pilot out of the craft when I saw the two panic-stricken Vietnamese soldiers running away. Their panic was about to cost them their lives, as the enemy would either kill or capture them. If we were to survive, we absolutely needed the radio and maps that these two soldiers were running away with. I shouted in Vietnamese for them to stop, but they would not. As the men and our radio were getting further and further away, I raised my M-16 and shot the radioman in the back of the head. There was little time to think about my action and there was no debate. In a matter of a few seconds I concluded that it was better for one man to die than to have the entire team perish in the jungle. The other soldier then stopped, turned around, and began to return. But, as expected, he was killed by the enemy before he could reach us. War is brutal. War is ugly. War is hell. Although I was deeply disturbed over taking the life of this soldier, I did what I had to do. I have thought of that situation countless times since then, and have concluded that given the same circumstances again today, I would make the same decision. We finally got the co-pilot out of the aircraft and quickly rigged it for demolition. We had gathered the equipment we would need to complete our mission, and were prepared to leave the area when I heard the familiar sound of an approaching helicopter.

I didn't know that a rescue chopper was only minutes from picking us up. I did not call for the choppers, and given the intense enemy gunfire, I would not have called them. They just showed up. I later learned that Shumate had sent them to verify our deaths. Two different pilots dropped in, at incredible risk to their own lives, and picked up my team. I climbed onto the second chopper, and we managed to fly out of there without being shot down again. The pilot, trying to protect me from being court-martialed for shooting the Vietnamese Ranger, reported that they fell out of the helicopter by accident. I appreciated his help, but preferred to tell the story like it happened. The next day I was debriefed on the events of the mission. The Vietnamese Ranger commander stared at me in wide-eyed disbelief when I reported that I shot one of his men. I had the full support of Special Forces Headquarters and the matter was dropped, but it did not take long for the word to circulate among the Vietnamese Rangers that if you were on a mission with a Delta recon team, you had better darn well follow instructions.

I had a two day break at Nha Trang, my face still sore from the blast of my own grenade on the five-day run. Despite this discomfort, however, my drinking was to kill the emotional pain, not the physical. The close range killing nightmare was still bothering me every time I fell asleep. The smell of death and sorrow and darkness was everywhere. I felt very much alone. When I lay awake, the recurring nightmare and the possibility of losing Barbara and my sons was constantly on my mind. Strong drink kept those bad feelings away while I was between missions. After the two day break, we were informed that there had been some heavy B-52 bombing along the Ho Chi Minh Trail. I was sent in with another Vietnamese Ranger team to assess that damage. We spent three days gathering and reporting damage information without enemy contact. The Vietnamese Rangers were particularly well-behaved.

During the last week of March, an A-team camp in the Ashau Valley was overrun by the enemy. Four Delta teams were sent into the area for a five-day mission to find survivors and to help with possible rescue. This was a good mission for me because my assigned area was away from the area where the enemy had been expected to be. Other Delta teams were placed into much more difficult situations. On the second day of the mission, we could hear Air Force fighters who had been called in by one of the other teams. One of the fighters was hit by enemy fire, and from the sound of the jet engines, it was clear that the aircraft was in trouble. I caught a glimpse of a parachute falling about a mile from us and was afraid the enemy could see it as clearly as we did. I felt sick at the thought of the enemy getting one more American pilot into their POW camps so we quickly made our way to find him. The area where he landed was mostly covered by tall trees into which his parachute descended and got hung up on the branches. As we arrived to the scene of the pilot hanging in the tree, we secured the area and found no sign of enemy activity in the immediate vicinity. It was comical to see that poor pilot hanging about fifteen feet from the ground. His .45 caliber handgun was clenched in both white-knuckled fists and his face was pale and sweaty. He was understandably scared stiff. I knew better than to make any movement toward him until I was able to convince him that we were Americans and were there to rescue him. I carefully moved around behind him so that he wouldn't shoot when he heard me, and then I called out, "Good morning, sir! I am with the United States Army. If you put that .45 away, I'll help get you down." The poor guy was tickled to death to hear my voice, and in a few minutes we helped him down and contacted Delta forward air control to send in a rescue helicopter. The chopper soon arrived but had to hover over the tall trees and drop a sling down for our pilot. We got the man into a rescue harness, then stuck his arm into the safety strap. He asked what the arm strap was for, and I explained that it would keep his body from falling to the ground if he was shot while on the way home. He didn't like hearing about getting shot at again and as he was pulled out of the trees by the chopper I noticed a blank stare on his pale face. It had only been about two hours since his aircraft had been shot down, and I'm sure those were the longest two hours of his life. It felt good to have a positive experience.

Two weeks later I was sent on a mission in the II Corps area, and was shot down for the fourth time. By then, I was totally worn out and tired of the blood, sorrow and killing. Chapter One of this book contains the story of that mission. During all of these months my family waited at home. I later learned that their lives were being damaged like mine, though in different ways. The boys were growing up without a father, or worse, with a father they loved and were continually frightened for. Mike later told me how they would sometimes sit quietly in the evening and one of them would start crying, out of loneliness for me, and the others would join in. It is a sad picture to think of them crying in one another's arms, waiting and hoping that I would return home safely. They watched and read news reports about the progress of the war and suffered their own hellish, emotional stress as they awaited word that I was alive, or perhaps that I had been killed. Too often there was news that one of my comrades had been killed, and then came the sorrow for the other wives and children as well as the feelings of guilt that their own husband and father was still alive. It was a lousy way to raise a family.

CHAPTER TEN
With Great Hope

During the first few months of this trip to Vietnam, when I expected to be killed before my year tour of duty was completed, I accepted the fact that I would not return home. After about six months, however, and after surviving some difficult situations, I began to wonder if I could possibly hold out for another six months. My early acceptance of imminent death was slowly replaced by a glimmer of hope that I might survive, after all. During the last six months in a war zone, most soldiers begin to feel a gut-wrenching anticipation about each mission. They think of the tragedy of being killed when only months, weeks, or even days away from their scheduled return home.

I had been sent on dozens of missions into enemy territory, nearly all of the missions resulting in blood and bullets. Only a sampling of those missions are told in this biography. None of this was fun or glorious or entertaining. Most of the experiences have been held back in my memory and rarely, if ever, discussed. It is too hard to explain to people who don't understand your feelings when you break down and weep over the memories. Too many people, who have never lived with combat experience, think of it as glorious and wonderful. Only those who are ignorant of reality think that way. War is hell and is hard to recall and discuss. The extremely intense experiences of battle leave deep emotional scars. I have discovered through the years that many of the people who tell war stories, to anyone who will listen, are less than genuine. Most who actually have intense experiences to tell, don't tell it. They can't. They spend their entire lives trying to push the memories as far back into their minds as possible. It was after several years of being prodded that I finally agreed to share some of these experiences with my son, Mike. These events took place more than thirty years ago, yet are still difficult to speak of. Too few American people recognize the sacrifices made by millions of their countrymen. We should do more to thank the mothers, fathers, wives and children of men who died in our defense, or who lived to carry the scars of combat. It is our duty to honor the wounded, respect the dead, and appreciate the unspeakable sacrifices of those millions who have paid the price to make this a country we can love. We must each live so as to be worthy of the efforts and sacrifice of those who have paid the price in our behalf. War is awful and miserable and must be avoided at all costs. Still there are times when good, decent people find that war is necessary. There is a monument to Special Forces veterans on a museum wall near Fort Bragg, North Carolina that says it best: "War is an ugly thing, but not the ugliest of things; The decayed and degraded state of moral and patriotic feeling which thinks that nothing is worth war is much worse. A man who has nothing for which he is willing to fight; nothing he cares about more than his own personal safety; is a miserable creature who has no chance of being free unless he is made free, and kept free, by the valiant exertions of men better than himself, for freedom is not free."

In June, Walter Shumate and I were at Cam Rahn Bay, waiting for a C-130 ride back to Nha Trang after a mission. Cam Rahn Bay had a major U.S. Navy port where materials and supplies poured in by the tons every day. As Shumate and I sat there on the airstrip waiting for our plane, we noticed a brand new Navy Volkswagen bus parked alongside the runway. It had been there for hours when we decided to walk over and examine it. Shumate noticed that the keys were in it, and asked me if I thought we could use a personal vehicle back at Nha Trang. We smiled mischievously. A few minutes later we were visiting the crew chief of the C-130 on which we were scheduled to fly. We explained to him that we had just negotiated the purchase of a Volkswagen bus, and asked if he had room to haul it inside the cargo bay of his plane. He was very helpful, and called the rest of his crew to help load the bus onto the plane. After an uneventful flight back to Nha Trang, we scraped the Navy markings off the bus, and enjoyed personal use of that vehicle for a couple of months before Navy investigators began asking questions about a missing bus. They had been tracking down the culprits who had stolen their bus and we figured that we only had a couple of days to get rid of it. We came up with a solution to two problems. There was a civilian Vietnamese man in Nha Trang who worked as an interpreter between the local American and Vietnamese troops. We had long known that he was a spy, so the information we relayed through him was never critical or secret, but was misleading. He was a real annoyance and we all talked of the day when he would get his reward. We found the interpreter one afternoon, and explained that we had an old bus for sale. We asked if he was interested in purchasing it. We knew that if we asked a low enough price, he would become greedy and after purchasing it, would quickly resell it for two or three times that amount. In a few hours the man returned with $300 cash with which to purchase the bus. We were pleased to accept his money, then immediately allowed him to drive it out of camp. The next day the spy/interpreter was caught selling the van, and was taken away by the police. We never heard from him, or the bus, again.

On one unusual mission four of us were sent on a tour of Taiwan, Singapore, Bangkok, Saigon and Hong Kong. President Johnson was taking a tour of these areas and our mission was to spend two days prior to President Johnson's visits to just watch and monitor any activity which might indicate that bad guys were planning on ruining Johnson's trip. If we saw anything unusual, we were to investigate and take action. We were given plenty of firepower. After Johnson showed up, the Secret Service took over and we went on to the next city. The Secret Service did not trust the police forces in those cities and depended on our knowledge and training to detect any assassination plots. We were given a free ride at some of the best hotels in Asia, and were given new, expensive suits and felt like rich folk. After staying a couple days in one city, observing the goings on in the same hotels that Johnson would stay in, we would then move on to the next city. We never detected any assassination plots, but we did enjoy the rest and relaxation. Most of the details of what we did on this mission and all the other missions, are still considered secret. You don't need to know, and I don't care to recall them.

One day a Bengal Tiger, complete with steel cage, showed up at the Delta Camp in Nha Trang. Someone had captured it, and had intended to make a profit by selling it. But, it had recently torn the arm off a man who was dropping some meat into its cage. The men had been told to get rid of it, but no one would take responsibility for it until it showed up in our camp where we were asked to kill it. Shumate and I thought we could skin the cat and tan the hide, but we did not want to shoot it and make a hole in the skin. Our plan was to put it to sleep with secobarbital. As a Delta medic, I had access to plenty of drugs and medications. I fed the tiger some hamburger with enough secobarbital to kill a six hundred-pound man, then waited for it to become drowsy. When it looked like the tiger was asleep, I reached into the cage and grabbed its tail, but was startled when the cat came to its feet and nearly crawled through the bars trying to reach me. Shumate and I scrambled away, tumbling over each other and falling to the ground with more danger of laughing ourselves to death than being mauled by the cat. Then Shumate said, "I'll tame that tiger so that even my little girl can pet it." He walked over to the cage, pulled his .38 Combat Masterpiece, and shot the tiger in the head. He had the skin tanned, and six months later his little girl did indeed have the 'tamed' tiger in her bedroom.

A month later, Shumate and I were sent on a mission into the mountainous jungles fifty miles north of Saigon. There had been several reports of up to eighty American soldiers seen in a POW camp in the area. Aerial photographs of the camp were inconclusive because of the heavy jungle canopy. This particular area was thick with enemy encampments and was generally avoided by helicopter flight because of the anti-aircraft fire. To avoid giving the enemy any idea that we were coming for a visit, we would not fly in by helicopter. We went into this mission by a High

Altitude/Low Open (HALO) parachute drop. We would be dropped out of an airplane at an altitude of over 30,000 feet, then free-fall almost all the way to the ground without opening our chutes. At the lowest possible altitude, the parachutes would be automatically deployed. To make the jump more secure, adding an unwelcome measure of excitement, we were to do this at night when there would be no chance of being seen by the enemy. Unless, of course, we landed in their camp. It is nearly impossible to drop from a plane six miles above the earth and then pinpoint a landing spot, especially at night. We didn't know for sure *where* we would land. Due to the high altitude, we wore warm clothing and oxygen masks, and due to the blackness of night, we wore infrared goggles and infrared markings on each other's parachutes. A big infrared 'X' on top of the parachutes was not visible to the naked eye, but *was* visible through the special goggles. We trained for the mission until we knew exactly what to do and where to go, then boarded a C-130 Hercules aircraft and flew to our drop zone. Shumate jumped first and I followed. HALO jumps are always interesting, but at night over enemy territory with absolutely zero visibility, this was especially exciting. I couldn't see Shumate--or anything else for that matter--and fell for a few minutes in total darkness before I was pleased to spot the big 'X' on his opened parachute. The night was very calm so the lack of wind was especially helpful. I went into a dive toward his position so that my chute might open nearly directly over him. When he landed, he was surprised to have me close enough to see just as he looked up for me. Before hiding our parachute equipment we waited silently for a over an hour to determine how close we might be to the bad guys. When we were sure that the area was safe, we hid our parachutes and cold weather gear, then carefully moved away from the landing site to spend the night in the jungle. It took us until noon the next day to orient ourselves. We had landed about ten miles from the POW camp. Our mission was to observe, return and report. We were not there to save anybody, but hoped to gather information that would eventually help us do just that. It was common to see civilians on our missions. We always avoided any contact with them, but there are hundreds of small villages and farms all over Vietnam. On this mission, we saw many more civilian farms than usual and every mile or so we would have to go out of our way to avoid being seen. We traveled carefully and slowly and it took us until the next afternoon to make our way to the camp. We were bitterly disappointed to discover that it had been abandoned and the prisoners moved only a few weeks before. We took pictures, then spent the next two days moving toward a secure area where we were picked up by helicopter.

Occasionally we would relax by going fishing, Delta style. We had a small outboard motorboat, and would take it into a small bay near Nha Trang with a couple of dozen grenades. One of us would run the boat in a wide circle while the other would toss grenades into the water. On the last trip around the circle, we picked up the dozens of fish that had been shocked and were floating on the water's surface. Fish fries on the beach were a favorite relaxation activity.

Another form of recreation was further training. Earlier in the year we had set up a jungle training course on an island off the coast of Nha Trang. At first the training course was for Delta recon members, but as the course became more sophisticated and impressive, General Westmoreland began inviting other Special Forces recon teams. Eventually, recon teams from the 1st Cavalry Division and others began training there. The United States had many well-trained soldiers, but at the time there were few soldiers with as much jungle warfare experience as the original Delta recon teams.

On October 7, 1966, I was finally finished with my tour. I was being rotated home, and for me the war was over. I said goodbye to my friends, many of whom I would never see again, and then waited for my flight. I had hoped for the day when I could return and make things right with my family and had already felt the anxiety of going on the last mission. As I sat around waiting for my ride out of Nha Trang, feeling anxious and fearful about my return to Barbara and the boys, a call came in that an American fighter pilot had been shot down just north of Cam Ranh Bay. The Air Force always called on Special Forces teams, especially Delta teams, when they had a downed pilot. We were glad to support them, because the Air Force pilots had saved our skins on many occasions. All other Delta recon team members were out on missions, except Alderman and myself. I had already turned in my gear and did not even have a weapon anymore, but there was no way I could say no thanks. A pilot was down and someone needed to retrieve him. I went to the armory for a weapon and obtained some gear, then together with Alderman and two Chinese Nungs we were briefed on the mission. As we prepared for this mission, my Sargent Major tried to convince me that I would be killed on this mission. There was a cruel sense of humor among the Delta folks. We loaded onto a UH-1 Huey chopper and flew to the area where the pilot had ejected from his aircraft. From the air, I found a suitable landing zone, and was directing the pilot when we began taking the familiar tracer machine gun fire from an enemy gun location to our right. All I could think was, *Here we go again!* The chopper pilot was hoping to get me to abort the mission, and yelled, "We're drawing fire from the right!" I was little comfort to him, as I said, "After you set us down, go left!" We landed and went to the exact location where the pilot should have been, but were disappointed to find no sign of him. We searched the entire area for two full days but we didn't ever find a trace of him. We saw a dozen enemy patrols, but never made contact with them as we searched for the pilot. We were disappointed to be airlifted out without him, and I have often wondered about his fate.

After surviving one last mission, this time I was really on my way home. I could hardly allow myself to think of Barbara and the boys. I wanted to race home and make things wonderful and happy again. So many difficult years had passed since I fell in love with my beautiful high school cheerleader. Could we be happy again? A small glimmer of hope remained with my heart, accompanied by the fear that it was too late.

Dear Daddy,

I am so happy our family is together again. It has been a long time since we were all happy. I remember the day you came home from Vietnam. You surprised us because we did not know you were on your way home. Joey came running up the porch and yelled "Daddy's home, Daddy's home!". I was mad at him because I thought he was teasing us about that and I yelled at him, but then I heard your boots walking on the porch. I hoped it was true for just a second and then you came into the doorway. I remember just running as fast as I could towards you and you kneeled down on one knee. I ran into your arms and you hugged me and picked me up. I will never forget that moment. I knew that finally everything would be all better and we could all quit being lonesome. I guess there is something wrong with you and mom, but I saw you ask her if she loved you and I saw her say yes. She was crying, but you were holding hands and I know everything will be okay. I was excited to move back to Ft. Bragg, but it was a long drive. I am so glad that we are together. Let's always be happy like this.

Love,
Mike

CHAPTER ELEVEN
The Closed Doors

I arranged to fly into Salt Lake City to see my mother, my sister Suell and brother Kin Jay. The reunion with my mother was sweet. She had prayed for my safety and longed for my return. Barbara and the kids were still in Anaconda, Montana and did not know that I had returned from Vietnam. I wanted to go and see them but I was afraid to discover that there was no hope to save the marriage. I feared losing my family more than I feared another year of the blood and sorrow of war. How would the reunion be? How would Barbara and I do together? Would I finally find that there was no marriage left? I felt to shrink rather than face the answers to these questions. I loved her and she loved me, so why was that not enough? In addition to these worries, the bitter memories of war and death I left behind in Vietnam, were constantly on my mind. I would often awaken through the night and wish that there was someplace to go where the memories couldn't follow. After a week of mental torment and unrelenting emotional anguish, I decided to make an unannounced trip to Anaconda. Once there, I would make every effort to reunite our family. I was certain I could get an assignment to the 10th Special Forces Group in Germany.

Still needing some time to regroup my thoughts, I rode the bus rather than a plane back to Montana. I spent all day on that bus with terribly mixed emotions. What would the reunion be like? Should I have called and announced I was coming? It had only been seven months since the close range killing that had affected me so severely that I still had not slept more than four hours at a time without being awakened by the awful image. So many of my friends had been lost. The bodies of Frank Badolati and Ron Terry were lying in the jungles of Bong Son. Would Barbara still want me? Could I ever find happiness? Finally, on October 19th, I arrived at the bus depot in Anaconda. While standing there waiting for my duffle bag to be unloaded, I glanced to my right and saw a familiar woman standing at the ticket counter. *It was Barbara.* I felt my heart leap into my throat. Coincidentally, she was there to ship a package at the very same moment of my unannounced arrival. It had been so long, and she was so very beautiful. In my surprise, I momentarily turned away because I didn't know how to approach her. Then, as she turned around, she noticed a Green Beret with polished boots standing near the bus. It must have taken her only a second to realize it was me, and she ran to me and called my name. I turned around and we fell into each other's arms. I could not let go of her as I felt a oneness with her that is impossible to describe. That moment has been frozen in my mind for thirty years, and is as clear today as it was when it took place. Neither of us could speak for a few minutes. We made quite a stir in the bus depot as the people read between the lines and understood what was happening. With both of us in a daze, Barbara drove me home so that I could see the boys Little Joe, who was five years old, was outside playing, and he saw me first. He turned and ran into the house to make the announcement. A moment later, I walked through the front door, and was thrilled when our oldest son, Mike, came running toward me. I fell to one knee, and he nearly knocked me over as he ran into my arms. Another moment frozen in time. Mike hugged me tight with his little arms around my neck. It had been so long since I had known such warmth. Then Joe came running into the room with Bobby. More wonderful moments. This was too good to be true. Why had I feared it? Never could I have dreamed that I could be experiencing the emotions that swept over me at this reunion with the four people I loved more than life itself. That day was spent in laughing and catching up, and my spirit had never felt so at peace. Barbara and I spent the next two days seriously discussing our future together. Because we had grown so far apart over the years, we both knew we had an uphill road to climb in getting our marriage back where it had been. We also knew that we were very different people now than we were ten years earlier when we were married. In spite of these differences, we both wanted desperately to make our marriage work. In one conversation, I asked her if she loved me. She said she *did* love me, and I expressed my love back to her. We shed tears, held hands and decided at that moment to move back to Ft. Bragg and wait for an assignment to Germany. At last, our family would again be together. We purchased a new 1966 Pontiac Grand Prix, then began a cross-country trip back to Ft. Bragg. While renting a house for a few weeks, we made arrangements to purchase our first home. We found the one we liked, and before long we had moved into our very own new house on Mango Circle, in Fayetteville, North Carolina.

Like a cancer that grows quickly and without warning, trouble continued to brew in our marriage. I was still a Green Beret assigned to an A-Team, and the training was never-ending. Long hours and many days were spent away from home, and life once again became lonely for both of us. In addition, I still carried the terrible scars of war, and grieved daily for the loss of good men whom I had loved. I simply couldn't get rid of the horrifying images of death that had been burned into my mind. Additionally, our assignment to Germany had been delayed. Try as we did, too many obstacles stood in the way of healing our marriage. Discontent escalated, angry words escaped, and tears ran down our cheeks. These painful tears pointed to our inevitable divorce. There were no magic pills, no magic wand, nothing we could do to give us hope. In February of 1967, with a very saddened heart, I purchased one-way plane tickets back to Montana for Barbara and the boys. We drove silently to the airport in Raleigh, and I said goodbye to my very reasons for living. I could scarcely speak without breaking down in tears; but before they left, I removed my watch and gave it to Mike. I told him to take care of everybody, and then without further words, I quickly turned and walked away. Mike, ten years old, stood in the airport corridor and cried aloud as he saw me go away. The pain in my heart was unbearable, for I knew the doors of happiness with my family had at last slammed shut. My marriage had finally failed, and try as I might, I simply couldn't go on.

While my thoughts were fumbling around in my mind, Barbara was seated in the plane, deep in her own thoughts. She remembers it this way: "I felt terrible inside. Leaving Bob was painful for us both, but I truly believe Bob was more devastated than was I. I recall looking out the plane window as we took off and gained altitude. There he was, standing alone on the tarmac. My heart fell as I saw his shoulders shaking, as he cried very, very hard. He was pretty tough, and I seldom saw him cry; but I will never forget that image for as long as I live. I just had to make a change, as I was becoming a total basket case, myself. My only relief, as I watched him grow smaller and smaller in the distance, was that he had never been abusive to the boys. He loved them, and he loved me."

Dear Daddy,

> *I still have the watch that you gave me at the airport, I will keep it forever. When will we get to see you again? School is okay, I guess. My fifth grade teacher is nicer than the teachers I had last year. Mom said we can come to see you at Christmas. I can't wait for that. Maybe by then everything will be okay and you and mom will be together again. We miss you a lot. I cried when I heard that Kin Jay died. We were all sad about that. Sometimes I just don't know how to feel. All I know is that someday our family needs to be together again. I can't wait to see you at Christmas.*

> *Love,*

> *Mike*

CHAPTER TWELVE
The Dark Ages

I had never felt so empty in my life. Even the sorrow and loneliness of war was no comparison to the emotional agony I faced during the next couple of months. While I was awake I had nightmares about losing my family, and while I was asleep I had the never-ending nightmares from the war. My Special Forces unit knew of my performance record in Vietnam, and they understood the sorrow I felt in losing my family. I was fortunate that they were compassionate and understanding, because I spent the next four weeks trying to drown my pain with alcohol. I fell to such depths that I even went absent without official leave, and got away with it. In fact, even the officer in charge of my unit, a very understanding Colonel, looked the other way. Whenever I was sober enough to remember who I was, I began to recall the bitter memories of my failed marriage. These thoughts would spin into others, and before long I would again drink myself into unconsciousness. From far-away Montana, Barbara was experiencing her own form of hell, and remembers it this way: "When Bob returned from Vietnam, he was understandably in a terrible mental and emotional condition. Because he had seldom shared any of the horrors of the war in his letters to me, I really didn't understand the depth of his problems when we were together in Ft. Bragg. If I had understood, I would hopefully have been more compassionate, or helpful. He had been through such harrowing and wrenching experiences that at the time I feared he would never again be the same."

One day Walter Shumate came to see me and we had a long talk. Shumate and I had been through a lot together, and he was a true friend. He was along side of me as we battled up the hill to save Hiner and Webber. I respected him and his counsel; so when he advised me to request a discharge from the military, I listened. Leaving the military was unimaginably difficult for me to do. It was like holding an expensive and beautiful vase, with strong sentimental attachments, and then smashing it to the floor. It seemed like such a waste of my training and capabilities. Nevertheless, my request was granted, and in March of 1967, I was honorably discharged from the United States Army Special Forces.

I suspect that I would have gotten myself straightened

out, and would have remained in the military, except for one thing: My 15-year-old brother, Kin Jay, had just been diagnosed with Leukemia, and had only a few months to live. Tragically, my mother had already lost two husbands and a son to death. Now, when I received word that she was about to lose another son, and knowing that she needed my presence and support, I felt that it was best for me to be discharged and move to her home, in Provo, Utah. By doing this, I could provide whatever solace and assistance I was capable of giving. As it turned out, it was my dear mother, even in her new anguish, who provided the solace for me. I needed that time with her as much as I needed the opportunity to regain a desire to keep living. By supporting my little brother in his last months, I was able to direct my energies toward service to him, rather than toward myself. In a very special way, his dying helped *save* my life. My brother Bill also came home to be with us during this time. Bill and I loved each other, and it was a joy to have him there. We spent time with mother, Suell, and Kin Jay, and we grew together again as a family. As I look back on those days, I see the hand of God, as He gave me comfort through my mother and siblings. Just before Kin Jay died, he asked for his Mormon bishop to give him a priesthood blessing. I thought the blessing was rather a strange custom of the Mormon faith, but I also appreciated how it seemed to comfort Kin Jay. He had been such a good young man, faithful in his church and having earned the rank of Eagle Scout, it seemed so awful for his life to be cut so short. My mother and the rest of the family were devastated about Barbara and me divorcing. They loved Barbara and my sons, and missed them terribly. The break-up of my family seemed to be especially hard on Kin Jay. Just before he died, he spoke with Suell and shared a powerful dream he had experienced the night before. In the dream, he had seen all of our family together again. He told Suell that even Barbara and I would some day be together again. He said he clearly saw us together, in his dream, and we were at a family reunion, with the boys, and we were swimming. Suell never forgot about Kin Jay's special dream of a family reunion. Although I didn't know it at the time, I now understand that it was a prophetic dream--a spiritual vision that was given to a righteous child of God to bless the rest of our family.

In June of 1967, my dear brother Kin Jay Galbreath quietly passed away. I had been on a three-day job in Los Angeles, and returned home the night he died. I was so torn up about his passing that I didn't, I couldn't, attend the viewing. I did go to his funeral, however, and was overwhelmed with sadness, both for myself in losing my younger brother at the prime of his life, and for my angel mother, who had already suffered so much. Kin Jay's suffering had been very difficult, but was finally over. The terrible sorrow that we had experienced, in losing him, served to awaken my senses. I tried to straighten up and accept the difficulties I faced--all without returning to alcohol. I was still hard-hearted, however, and I remember being angry with my mother who was paying 10 percent of her meager income to the Mormon church. She had very high hospital bills with Kin Jay's illness, and she had to support herself, but still she gave to the church. I was upset about that for a long time, and even sat down with her bishop to criticize him for taking money from a widow. I wondered how the church could do any more good with her money than she could do for herself.

While he assured me that she was simply being obedient to a commandment from God, and that the church would certainly take care of any needs she might have, still my heart did not soften. From where I stood, it simply made no sense. It had been a little more than a year since I had experienced the close-range killing in Vietnam. I still hadn't slept a single night without waking up with nightmares of that event. The brutality of war was still difficult to live with, especially since I had begun to question the purpose of it. I joined the local Veterans of Foreign Wars group, in Provo, and did find some comfort there. Some of these people had experienced similar trauma in war, and we felt comfortable with one another.

Often I thought of calling Barbara, and of trying to get back together. I thought that since I was now out of the military, just maybe we could make our marriage work. She was always on my mind, although never once did I have the confidence to approach her on the subject. As the months wore on, I slowly lost all hope of ever having Barbara again. When I thought too much about it, I would find myself at the local bar, trying to forget what was bothering me. Every few months I would hear from Shumate, and he would let me know which of our friends had most recently been killed. I often wished that I had been among those killed. Death would have been a much easier thing to handle than being alive on the outside, while being dead on the inside.

For a Christmas present to my sons, I purchased airplane tickets for Mike, Bobby and Joe to come to Provo for a week. As Christmas of 1967 approached, I was like a little boy waiting for Santa Claus. The anticipation of seeing

118

them again, and of spending a week with them, was the most exciting thing that had happened since I had talked the downed pilot into coming down out of the tree. Finally, the day of their flight arrived. I picked them up at the airport in Salt Lake City, and we talked, laughed, and told stories well into the night, renewing the father-son friendship that had so long been dormant. During the next week, Mike began asking questions that eventually led to the big question. "Dad," he asked timidly, "can I stay here and live with you? I've been away from you almost my entire life. Please let me stay with you." I was warmed deep inside by Mike's desire to be with me, and so after assuring him that I would speak with his mother about it, he went to bed. Later that night, I called Barbara, and we spoke for some time about Mike's request. She understood Mike's feelings, and his desperate need for a father, and agreed to let him stay with me. Bobby and Joe had a difficult time understanding this arrangement, but they accepted it. Obediently, they returned to their home in Montana. Mike and I, meanwhile, began a new life together in Provo.

I enrolled Mike as a fifth grader at Franklin School in Provo. We stayed in my mother's apartment, and shared the same bedroom. For the next two years we played catch, tried tennis, went hiking, attended school plays, played chess and enjoyed one another. Those were special days, indeed, but sorrow still seemed to be a constant companion. One day we received a telephone call from Barbara, informing us that she had just remarried. Mike had talked of our family being reunited, and had hoped with all his heart for it to happen. It is hard on young hearts and for Mike this news was confusing and disappointing. Barbara's remarriage seemed to cut the final thread of hope as it dashed my newly found happiness. I gradually returned to the numbing effects of alcohol. Occasionally I would hear Mike crying late at night and my heart would break for him. He asked me once if I thought miracles could really happen, but I didn't realize what he was referring to. I told him that I thought most miracles we hear about aren't true and to not depend on them. I remember another time that he seemed depressed and told me, "it seems like nothing is right". I didn't know how to respond to that, because I felt the same way.

Two years passed, and in February of 1970, Mike decided it was time for him to return to live with Barbara and his brothers. By this time, I had moved him around the country, and he was missing a lot of school. It was his decision to go, and although it caused me great sorrow, I supported his decision. It was the right thing to do. However, it seemed to open the floodgates of some of my pent-up emotional struggles. My drinking became even heavier. Although I didn't know it at that time, I was an alcoholic. I set up a drinking schedule, and would drink when I knew I could, then stay sober when I knew I had to. I worked on construction jobs and in the oil fields, and was always able to go to work sober, knowing that I could drink later. I had been smoking cigarettes for years. My mother had encouraged me to stop, but I would snap back at her about how I could spend my money as I pleased, just as she could spend her money on the Mormon church as she pleased. During the occasional telephone calls and our summer visits, I could tell that the boys were getting hard feelings about the whole situation. Mike began fighting and getting in trouble, and the other boys followed. I felt that I had failed them.

Another year passed . . . then two . . . then five. My teeth were becoming more and more of a problem because of the shrapnel still embedded in my mouth. I tried to get them fixed at a Veterans Hospital, but there was no record of my having been wounded in the mouth. Delta was somewhat distanced from the regular army units and the records were either not kept well, or were classified and not available. For whatever reason, the Veterans hospital said the shrapnel must have come from somewhere else besides a war zone, so I was left on my own to keep my teeth repaired. As late as 1990, the x-rays showed a dozen bits of steel, but still no help from the VA. I have an eight inch scar on my hip from a bullet at Plei Me, a six inch scar on my ankle from a bullet north of Pleiku, shrapnel scars on my back from north of Bien Hoa, and bits of steel in my teeth and gumbs from my own grenade in the Srepok river basin, but no paperwork was available to show that it was service connected, so I still pay for the health care myself.

As the dark years passed, each summer I would see the boys for a couple of weeks, and each night I would drink so that I could sleep without thinking or dreaming of my loneliness. Seldom did a day pass without thinking of Barbara and the boys. Six more years passed as the boys began to grow into men. Mike had joined the Army and was stationed in Hawaii. During this time, Mike had married and when their first son, Jarom, was born, I became a proud grandfather. I loved all three of my sons and thank goodness they all stood beside me as their father. This was my one ray of hope, in an otherwise dismal and lonely existence. One day I felt particularly alone after a long quiet weekend. I decided to call each of the boys, and spoke to each of them for about ten minutes, then hung up and sat on the edge of the bed in my small apartment. I felt lonely and depressed but tried to avoid drinking my sorrows away. I wanted to feel better somehow. I tried not to cry, but the hurt was too deep so, as I sat on the edge of my bed, I wept.

Occasionally, while seeing the boys during the summer, I would see Barbara, and we would get a chance to talk. Those conversations were always difficult, and I held back the tears whenever we parted. My alcoholism had been joined by another illness--that of depression. One day I sat by myself, stone sober, and realized that I was not happy, and that I had spent most of the last twenty years *without* happiness. Even when I had my family with me, as well as the two years when I had Mike with me, I was not truly happy. What had been missing? Was it the war? Had my wartime experiences ruined my capacity to be happy? Could I ever *find* happiness? Did *everyone* feel this way? Could I ever be happy, under any circumstances, without Barbara? These questions, and others, churned over and over in my mind, and always I came back to the same common denominator, Barbara. Although I knew that I, alone, was responsible to make myself happy, still my love for her was the fuel that fed the fire inside me that had been almost extinguished for so long. Shortly after Mike had joined the Army, he was taught about the Mormon church by two missionaries, Elder Judd and Elder Quinney. He gladly accepted the gospel message and became an active Mormon. He seemed to be happy with his conversion, but I could not really understand his feelings. Mike spoke to me of his newly found faith and membership in the Mormon Church. He said that his hard feelings had been melted away by the gospel, and he spoke of peace and hope and happiness. I did not even know what those words meant. Not long after Mike became a faithful Mormon, he taught Barbara the gospel and she also joined herself with the Mormons. Then Joe became active in the church, and then Bob. All these people, whom I loved, were all becoming Mormons. What was all this Mormon nonsense? What did they find so attractive in this church? None of it made any sense to me.

Dear Daddy,

A lot of years have passed. It hardly seems real to me that I am married and in the Army. I wanted to send these pictures of your first grandson, Jarom Michael Wren. Jarom is an unusual name, I know, but since I joined the Mormon Church, I wanted to give him a name that will always remind him of this great Church. The name comes from the Book of Mormon and it has special meaning to me.

I have believed in God all of my life, even when I was so young that I did not really know who He was. I hope someday that you try to discover the peace and hope and happiness that can be yours through the gospel of Jesus Christ. A wonderful series of miracles brought me to this Church and I pray that the same miracles can help you understand how I feel. I think about you every day. I think about Mom every day, too. I will see you at Christmas when I am home on leave.

Love,
Mike

CHAPTER THIRTEEN
The Light of Christ

I knew Mike, his brothers and Barbara had hope and faith, and that they were living life the way I should have lived it. This gave me some portion of hope, although I really didn't know what to do with that hope. Somehow, though, I was not ready and continued to find solace in drinking. During the school year of 1977-1978, Joe decided to move from Anaconda to live with me during his junior year of high school. He had joined the Mormon church the same time as Barbara only a year earlier, and I thought he was having second thoughts about it. At first I figured he might have moved down to be with me where he thought the standards might be more relaxed and where he could run around and misbehave a bit. I was surprised, and even proud of him, as he got up each Sunday and found his way to a Ward and got active in his youth group. His activity in the Church was something that I very much admired, though I wouldn't begin to admit that to anyone. Often we would spend Saturday mornings at a breakfast restaurant or donut shop. Joe would always say something of a spiritual nature and I would pretend to have ignored it. Sometimes guilty feelings would swell up deep within me and remind me of the wrongs I had done throughout my life. It hurt to think of spiritual things. It hurt to think that I could never be like Barbara and the boys, and actually be forgiven. Afraid to approach God to ask his help, I sometimes wondered if He would ever help me be happy. I was glad my sons were happy in their lives, but I never believed that happiness would be mine. In depression and loneliness, with beer as my constant companion, I struggled through the years, waiting for the few wonderful days each year when I could see my sons and their families. As the months and years dragged by, my depression grew deeper.

Some years later, in May of 1983, Mike spent several weeks with me at my home in Bakersfield, California while he searched for employment there. He was attempting to move his family there where we could be together more often. Unfortunately, there was no suitable work available so Mike prepared to return to his wife and children in Montana. Seventeen years had passed since I left Vietnam, and another fifteen years had passed since Barbara had remarried. Bobby and Joe were now grown, and had likewise married, and I was now the proud grandfather of ten beautiful grandchildren. Bob's wife Lorene, Joe's wife Nancy, and Mike's wife Sharon, were all I could have hoped for in daughters, and I was so proud to be called 'Dad' and 'Grandpa'. I loved being with my family, but I had to be careful and not smoke or drink around them. I wanted happiness, I wanted peace, and I wanted hope. Although Mike had said that he had found these gifts within his Mormon Church, I just didn't feel that religion was for me. As people spoke about God and the church I was always afraid to ask the question about forgiveness. I knew enough about the Bible to know that God had commanded that men must not kill one another. Somewhere I learned that killing was unforgivable. I felt that I was beyond hope of forgiveness and dared not ask to find out for sure. I felt that I had done so much wrong in my life that there was no hope for me. It seemed that it was too late to change, and that if there was a God, he surely could not care for me like he cared for others. I was neither good enough nor important enough for Him to care about me. The sorrow I had caused my family and the foolish things I had done through the years made me ashamed of myself. While Mike was there to visit me, he attended church, and one day he asked me if I had any scriptures. I dug through some old things that my mother had saved for me. In those things was a leathered copy of a Book of Mormon that my mother gave to me in 1949 at my baptism. Because it was old, and because my mother had saved it for me, I felt a sentimental attachment to that book, though I had never read a word from its pages. I showed the book to Mike and he opened it to several verses in Chapter 32 of a book called *Alma*. The verses spoke of faith. They described how a person could develop faith even if all he had was a *desire* to believe. I truly wondered if having a desire would work for me. I did not want the Mormon Church, I only wanted peace and happiness . . . and most of all, *hope*. Mike marked those verses and asked that I read them. At the end of his three week visit with me, I was terribly saddened to see him prepare to leave. I fought back the tears as we said good bye, and knew of the loneliness that I would feel when he was gone. I couldn't bear to think of it. I traveled home with such a heavy and lonely heart that it was one of the most sorrowful times of my life. Though depression had become my worst enemy, the day he left, I thought of the scripture in Alma over and over again. Dare I try the experiment of faith? The thought pounded at me, in my heart, again and again. At three o'clock the following morning, I got out of bed, turned on the light, and read the verses again. The words somehow seemed to draw at my heart. About a week later, with the same questions haunting me, I opened the Book of Mormon again, and read the same verses. Could I develop faith? The verses in Alma 32, finally worked their way into my heart. I began to know that I had to change. It became clear to me that the first thing I needed to do was to stop drinking. It became clear that I was an alcoholic, and I finally had confessed to myself that I needed help. Until I read these scriptures, I had not really wanted to change. It was the verses about faith, in the Book of Mormon, together with the spirit of truth, that gave me the motivation to search for help. I found a hospital that treated alcoholics. They wanted $1,500 for each week of treatment, but I sincerely felt my life was worth the investment. I owned a welding truck that was worth many thousands of dollars, but I didn't want to take the time to get the best price for it, so I sold it for $1,500 to the first man who came along to purchase it. I took the money, drove straight to the hospital, and had myself admitted. By the end of a very intense week of therapy, I had learned a great deal about myself. The doctors and counselors emphasized over and again that alcoholism was an incurable disease. They said that I would fight the disease for the rest of my life. The counselor taught me that there was only one person who could really help me change. He said that change could only come from within *myself*. I couldn't afford another week in the hospital, so I left with a resolve to never again allow alcohol to enter my mouth. They had given us a copy of a small book called One Day at a Time that gave a spiritual thought for each day. No matter how we felt, we were to read that thought each day. I did so faithfully for months. One day as I read from the small book, the thought came to me that I should read from the Book of Mormon as Mike had encouraged me to do. After reading for a week or two, I determined that I was not learning enough, so I went to visit my brother, Bill, who very sympathetically listened to my story. He expressed his vote of confidence, then gave me a copy of the Holy Bible that was sitting on his shelf. The next several months were spent trying to find meaning in my life, and to try the experiment of faith which I read of in Alma 32. I made a determination to read every day from the Bible that Bill had given me, and from the Book of Mormon and then something wonderful began to happen. Little flickers of joy would occasionally dash through me, and I began to feel little moments of peace. What was happening? I would wake up in the morning and feel a glimmer of joy and then have confidence that I could make it through another day without drinking. Small things began to change in my life as I continued to read from the scriptures each day. I began to smile and feel good about my future. I felt peace, little by little. After reading faithfully every day for a year, and having not had a drop of alcohol since leaving the hospital, life began to look much different to me. I arose each morning with a sense of purpose, and began to work on a project that, for years, had been but a dream. I purchased an old oil field that had a dozen broken-down oil wells on it. The wells had not produced oil for years, but I felt that with a lot of hard work I could get them to produce enough oil to make a good living. The oil property was sixty miles from Bakersfield, so I sold nearly everything I had, then purchased a small house trailer to live in while working on the oil wells. It was back-breaking work in Bakersfield heat, but I was proud of what I was accomplishing. Still reading scriptures every day, the thought came to me that I should try going to church, so occasionally I would drive into town on Sundays and attend one of the local Mormon wards. I listened to the talks in Sacrament meeting and learned a great deal from what I heard. I did not have any friends there and seldom spoke to anybody. My Indian skin had been made even darker by the years of outdoor work and I probably was a bit scary to all the well-dressed Mormon folks. I still hadn't had a drink of alcohol since leaving the treatment center.

Thoughts about praying began to occur to me. I was unsure about prayer and wondered if I was too bad of a person to pray to God. I felt I was unforgivable and too unworthy to ask for His help. People often have a hard time forgiving themselves, and so it was with me. The prompting to kneel and pray for help was powerful and eventually I made the attempt to pray for help to be a better person. One evening, out on my quiet little oil field, all alone in my small trailer house, I kneeled down, for the first time in my life, and begged forgiveness. At first, I felt ashamed to even ask, but my shame was over shadowed by the Saviors love. The warmth of God's love poured over me and tears washed down my face as peace filled my heart. The burden of sin was lifted from me and I knew that Jesus Christ, the Redeemer of Israel, had paid the price for me. The blood of the Lamb had been spilt for all people, but for the first time in my life I recognized that the atonement included me. After so many tears of sorrow, it was the first time in my life that I shed tears of joy. The Lord had been trying to express His love for me, for all of my life, but I couldn't hear through my pride and drinking. Now, things would be different for me. Every night I kneeled in prayer and then read from the scriptures. The verses I read were my strength for the next day. And, after more than a year of work, I began to have success in my business venture. Oil was being produced from wells that people said would never produce again. Mike had been discharged from the Army several years earlier, and was about to graduate from college. He and his wife Sharon, with their eight children, would soon arrive in Bakersfield to live and they were depending on me to help get them settled. In October of 1985, I sold my first tank of oil. The production was much better than I expected, and it became clear that my income from the sale of oil would exceed $30,000 monthly. In the next couple of months I began to pay off the debts against my oil property, and by spring of 1986, I would be ready for

Mike and his family to arrive and begin their lives at my side. I was excited to have them coming and expected to have sufficient income for myself and all my sons and their families. I beamed with happiness every morning, as the scriptures and prayer replaced the alcohol and loneliness.

My great expectations were soon dashed, however. In January of 1986, the worldwide oil industry began to feel the effects of an oil glut. The price of Kern River crude oil had dropped from $22 per barrel down to $4 per barrel. In a matter of a few weeks everything that I had worked on for two years was falling apart on me. My little oil field was now worthless. I watched the news every day for some sign of a turn in the industry, but it only got worse. Almost overnight I was unable to sell my oil, or to pay my debts. By April, I was facing the loss of the oil property that I had spent so much effort developing. I called my debtors and explained that I would hang on for six months and if things did not turn around I would sell everything and make sure they were fully paid. In a couple of months Mike and his family would be with me, and I was becoming concerned about what I would do for them.

I did not think things could get much worse until one day in May when I returned to my oil property and found that my house trailer had accidentally caught fire. It had burned to the ground, taking everything I owned with it. Everything I owned was now in ashes or was worthless. The financial stability I had anticipated for so long had suddenly crumbled right before my eyes. The oil property was about to be lost to debtors because I couldn't sell the oil, and my home had gone up in smoke. I owned nothing, I had no income, and now I was homeless. I still thank God that the triple combination Book of Mormon which mother had saved for me for so many years was not in the trailer, but was at my side when everything else burned to the ground. Hope was not lost, however, because I still believed in the verses in the Book of Mormon that I had read daily for the previous two years. God directed me to search for His kingdom first, and then promised that all other things would be given to me. He said that He would clothe even the grass of the fields, and I knew that I was more important than grass. A miracle had truly taken place. All earthly possessions had been taken from me, but I now desired to search the scriptures for hope, rather than to turn to alcohol in despair. Joy had replaced depression. My daily prayers had given me hope that I could be forgiven of my sins and that Heavenly Father understood me. I still did not know very much about the doctrine of the church, but I loved what I read from the scriptures. The peace and hope and happiness that everyone spoke of were actually becoming reality for me. Still, this was a time of testing for me like I had never before known. I have since learned that Heavenly Father expects things from each of us that we often do not know we can give. Anybody can search the scriptures and kneel in prayer when they think they are about to be wealthy. What our Father in Heaven wanted to know was, would I still be praying and searching for His word when all earthly things were taken from me? I had spent a lot of time under enemy fire, this time it was my faith that was under fire. With the grace of God, I survived both trials.

I moved into town and got a job processing oil for

someone else just as I had been doing for myself. I had a steady income, and I found a house for Mike and Sharon and their family, who would be arriving in just a week. Bob and his family were living in Fresno, and I was pleased to often enjoy their company. Joe and his family were still living near Barbara, in Montana. The doors that had closed on me nearly twenty years earlier were suddenly beginning to re-open. My heart, even though a part of it was still empty, was suddenly swelling with joy. Barbara had become a faithful member of the church, and I wondered if she felt as good as I did. During these years I had been an occasional visitor at the local ward. The members there were friendly, but this grizzled old Blackfeet Indian was a bit rough around the edges, so I didn't have much social life with them. However, when Mike and his family arrived, we began to attend regularly, and I found myself learning even more about living the gospel. I had read from the scriptures every day of the last three years. One day Mike gave a talk in sacrament meeting about tithing. He spoke of some of the difficult days he and his family had endured while trying to get through college with eight kids. He said that he couldn't imagine how anybody could go through life and not depend on the blessings of obeying the law of tithing. At that moment I felt ashamed that I hadn't even thought of paying tithing earlier. I resolved then and there to pay a full tithe for the rest of my life. What's more, I knew mother had been right all those years earlier--paying tithing *was* the right thing to do. I still spoke with my mother often and she was thrilled and relieved at my new interest in the church. While staying with Mike and his family, I spoke with my first grandson, Jarom, and asked if he had ever read the Book of Mormon. He said that he was in the middle of reading it and challenged me to read with him. I started again from the beginning and read every day. In a playful race with Jarom, we finished two weeks sooner than we had planned. Looking back it is clear that the Lord was teaching me 'line upon line, and precept upon precept' as I was ready to receive it. I often thought of how my knowledge and testimony of Jesus Christ had changed my life. I wished that I could go back in time and make the gospel a part of my life when I was young and then grow up without so many regrets. How I wished that I had listened to what my mother tried to teach me at the time of my baptism. I wanted to do good continually, but a life without the gospel makes the pursuit of excellence much steeper for late-bloomers, like me. Oh, the good I could have done throughout my life, if I had asked the Lord's help sooner. Had my foundation been built upon the Rock of our Redeemer, who is Christ, the Son of God, I would not have spent so many decades in the gulf of misery (Helaman 5:12). By my own stubbornness, I brought misery upon myself. I vowed to build my foundation upon the teachings of the Savior, just as Barbara and my sons had already done. I have been referred to as a war hero, a title that I abhor. The real heroes in this life are the young men and women, and others, who give of themselves to serve missions and testify of Christ, the Savior of the world.

While reading from the Book of Mormon, it occurred to me that most people do not recognize the horror, and tears, and depth of sorrow that is contained in so many Book of Mormon events. When the narrator briefly states that thousands of Lamanites were slain, or that circumstances forced the execution of prisoners, no mention is made of the emotional pain suffered by those who did the slaying. There is no record of the lifelong sorrow and guilt and nightmares of a man who watched another person die by his hands. There is nothing written of the terror of battle, in a kill-or-be-killed situation, or of the tragic sorrow the men suffered after slaying frightened prisoners, or of the endless nights of torment trying to forget what they did. War is ugly, war is brutal and war is hell. Every effort must be made by all people everywhere to pray for peace.

One day I was visiting with a long-time friend of mine--a friend who was unaware that it had been several years since I had taken a drink. He opened a can of beer and placed it in front of me. As I stared at it, tears formed in my eyes. Not until this very instant did I realize I was healed of my alcoholism. I had no desire, whatsoever, to take a drink. While I sat there, a wonderful spiritual witness came over me, and I clearly saw that the hand of God had carried me through the last two years. Heavenly Father loved me! He loved *me*, an old Blackfeet Indian who had done so much wrong in this life. I felt wonderfully warm and good at that moment as I quietly said, *"No, thank you"* to my friend. To avoid crying right in front of him, I went into the restroom and sat there weeping tears of gratitude for what Heavenly Father had done for me. The doctors had told me that alcoholism was an incurable disease, yet I had not tasted alcohol since the day I left that hospital. With God all things are possible.

In May of 1987, Barbara came to Bakersfield to visit Mike and his family. I had not seen her for so many years but found her just as beautiful as she had been all those years before as my new bride. I had to struggle to keep my emotions in control as we visited together with our children and grandchildren. She had flown down from Montana for an emotional break because she was in the middle of a divorce. Her husband had been an abusive alcoholic for years, but she avoided divorce because, with her newfound faith, she felt that divorce was morally wrong and had struggled with that marriage for years trying to do what was right. She endured the physically abusive relationship as long as she could, but was now ending her marriage. She spent two weeks there in Bakersfield, and we enjoyed a nice visit. When it was time for Barbara to return to her home in Montana, we stood together for a moment on the porch. I looked into her eyes and saw something special. I saw the girl I had known as a cheerleader all those years ago. I looked into her soul and remembered the days when we loved each other and stood together as husband and wife. We stared into each other's souls for but a moment and when she left I began to feel again some of the pain of our unhappy separation more than twenty years earlier.

After her divorce, Barbara remained in Montana for another year before returning to Bakersfield. I thought she enjoyed seeing me again and that she would come back to Bakersfield immediately after her divorce, so I became discouraged when she didn't return. I had hoped she would come down to live near me and that we would live happily ever after. After seeing her and visiting with her under the light of the gospel, and getting my hopes up, the fall to reality was too much to bear. Feelings of depression, then despair, crept slowly into my heart. I moved into my own apartment, and gradually stopped reading from the scriptures and attending church. Though I did not return to alcohol, I did begin to fail, spiritually. I wanted so much to have Barbara return, and this longing desire quite literally consumed my thoughts. My faith was again under fire. I was living a flashback of those decades of loneliness and despair. Years of living without the gospel had taken a terrible toll on me. Try as we do, perfection is a lofty goal that comes slowly, especially for me. I continually beg the Lord's patience and forgiveness. One evening Mike came to my apartment and we had a nice visit. I could tell that there was something on his mind, and he asked if we could go for a short drive. He told me about a terrible dream that he recently experienced:

Dear Daddy,

I want to tell you of a dream that I had a few nights ago. It was a terrible dream which has left me very disturbed. I dreamed that I heard you come into my home and begin to come down the hall toward me. Before you reached me, I heard you fall down. As I ran to the hall to see what had happened, I saw you lying collapsed on the floor. A fear came over me as I lifted your head into my lap, and I saw you die in my arms. It was such a devastating feeling that I cannot fully describe it. The feeling came to me that your physical death would be tolerable to me, but your spiritual death would be more than I could bear. You are my best friend. Your spiritual welfare is critical to our eternal happiness. Please pray for strength to endure to the end.

Love,

Mike

Mike's dream dealt with my spiritual death, and it served as a catalyst to start me back on the right path. I began once again to read from the Book of Mormon every day, and I returned to Church. Being without Barbara, after seeing her the previous year, was more than I could stand. Even so, I had to re-learn a lesson that had so impressed me a year earlier. Heavenly Father wanted to know if I would still pray and study the scriptures, and strive for righteousness, *even if all was taken from me*. It was another test of my faith. I had failed that test, but when I realized this, I vowed to never fail in faith again. I visited with my bishop, and he helped me understand more principles of the gospel. At the time, I believed that my blessings were due to the goodness of those around me. These included my mother, my sister, my brother and sons--but not because of *me*. The bishop helped me understand that all blessings were based on obedience to commandments. This was a sweet revelation to me . . . to think that Heavenly Father found me worthy of my own blessings. I thought these blessings were from righteousness of other people, and that I was enjoying what others had earned. Was God truly finding *me* worthy of His generosity? Somehow, through His gift of grace, I knew that He was. I had read the words in the scriptures that said unto whom much is given, much is required. I now understood that if I was being so blessed, I was required to return the blessings to the Lord. To accomplish this, I resolved to place myself in the service of others. For me, there *was* no greater gift. Or, so I thought at the time-- What I *didn't* know was that, even then, the Lord was preparing my heart to receive the grandest blessing of all.

CHAPTER FOURTEEN
Always On My Mind

Life was wonderful. I loved my new faith and enjoyed associating with saints. Mike and Bob, with their families, were close and my decades of loneliness had ended. The peace and hope and happiness which Mike had told me of some fourteen years earlier, were now a reality for me. The terrible scars of war had faded and were replaced with the Light of Christ. In June of 1989, Barbara packed all of her belongings and moved to Bakersfield. She lived with Mike and Sharon for six months while she searched for a job. I didn't see her during any of that time . . . simply because I was afraid to. It was a self-preservation thing. If I had enjoyed time with her, and then found that I had to be without her again, it would have killed me. To look into her eyes and see the beautiful woman I had loved for so long, and then to lose her, would have left scars deeper than those of war. For those first six months, I simply could not be in her presence.

The following January, twenty three years after placing Barbara and the boys on the plane in Raleigh, North Carolina, I somehow mustered up the courage and asked Barbara for a date. She seemed glad to accept, and we had a nice time over dinner. Lingering at the restaurant, we talked until late into the night, and shared our feelings about the gospel to one another. The following morning I was so excited to see Barbara again that I called and asked her on another date. Then another . . . and another. Oh, how I loved being with this beautiful person. We spent nearly every day together.   We walked and talked, and visited our grandchildren. We laughed and enjoyed movies and picnics, and we fell in love . . . again. When we finally got around to speaking of the hurt and the divorce, and the reasons for it all, we both understood one another's feelings. There were no hard hearts, and there were no harsh feelings. The gospel of Christ had prepared our hearts for this wonderful reunion. One beautiful evening, while we were together, she looked into my eyes and said, "You were always on my mind." There cannot possibly be a joy in this life that is greater than the joy I felt at that moment, as we embraced and allowed the tears to roll down our cheeks.

In June of 1990, a family reunion was held. Barbara and her sister and mother, my brother Bill and his family, my mother and Suell and dozens of other people came. The reunion lasted several days as we talked and laughed and renewed friendships that had long been lost. One afternoon we were all at Buena Vista Lake near Bakersfield and were enjoying a picnic. I was at the barbecue grill and all the kids were swimming and laughing when my sister, Suell, gathered us together and, with tears in her eyes, she reminded us of Kin Jay's dream just before he died twenty three years earlier. Kin Jay had told of the dream he enjoyed wherein Barbara and I were back together again at a family reunion and we were swimming. Our eyes swelled with tears as we enjoyed the witness of the Holy Spirit that his dream was truly from God.

It was almost too much to comprehend as we began to plan our wedding. Announcements were made to many happily surprised people. Tears of joy were a daily occurrence as we made plans for our special day. The hour finally arrived for our marriage and I think we were more nervous than we had been the first time. Still, we were there with family and friends, and all Barbara and I could think of was how wonderful it was to have our family reunited. I did not yet feel ready to go to the temple, so Barbara and I were to be married by her Bishop and planned for a year later to have our marriage solemnized in the temple. On the day of the wedding, Mike and I drove together to the chapel. It was a beautiful autumn afternoon. We arrived an hour early and had plenty of time to sit in his car and reflect on what had transpired through the last thirty years. Mike told me of two special prayers which he had offered during those troubled years. He told me of the times he had knelt down as a little boy, while I was in Vietnam, and prayed that I would not be killed. He told me of his fear that I would be run over by a tank, and how the Lord comforted him. I listened and marveled at how a youngster with no training in prayer, would ever think to call on God for help. A wonderful and spiritually intense testimony overcame each of us as we sat in that car. I finally understood that God had truly protected me because of the sincere and faithful prayers of my family and of a frightened little boy. Tears fell in both our eyes as the Holy Spirit witnessed to us both that the hand of God had carried me through those bloody days. I had been shot down four times, once in balls of flame, I had been blown up, shot, diseased, wounded, starved, and given ample other opportunities to perish. The simple faith of prayer had protected me. Why? For the blessings of that very moment, and to show to the world that in His own season, God hears and answers the worthy prayers of His children. Mike also told me of the prayer which had been uttered through his tears as he knelt down as an eleven year old boy and asked that God bring his mom and dad together again. That prayer stayed in his heart for more than twenty years and was only an hour from being answered. There were more tears as we expressed our love and admiration for one another. A short time later Barbara and I were married . . . again. The wedding was wonderful and filled with close relatives who each acknowledged the blessings of God in that sacred event. Our three faithful sons, and their wives and children, were the honored guests at their parents reunion.

In September of 1992, Barbara and I, together with our sons and their families, met in the Las Vegas Temple to be sealed as husband and wife for eternity. As Barbara recalls, "It felt so good to know that the sons I love were the same sons my husband loved. The same things I had grown to love--the Savior, Jesus Christ, and His truths, were part of Bob's life now, as well, and we had such strong feelings of unity and love. It felt right, it felt good, and it felt proper. It was an enormous blessing to be able to begin again, this time with the gospel in our lives to guide and unite us. To be married in the temple was something I had looked forward to since my conversion to the Church in 1976. For all of us, this day was a dream come true, and our tears flowed freely. But no tears flowed more freely than Mike's, as this was a culmination of decades of hopes and wishes and prayers for his parents. He never gave up hope that we would be together again. Now, as Bob and I knelt hand-in-hand at the altar, we felt like we were in heaven! Such gratitude was ours, for repentance and forgiveness, for the grace of our Savior,

Jesus Christ. It was because of a very tiny exercise of faith, that something so wonderful as this actually happened. Our joy was full to over-flowing."

Dear Daddy,

I need to thank you and mom for the blessing you have both been to me in my life. Your example and dedication to family, country and church have been an inspiration to me. Your long awaited, yet vigorous, acceptance of the gospel has been an answer to many prayers. Who would have dreamed that you and mom could be brought together after so many years?

I will be forever grateful for the wonderful memory of you and Mom kneeling at the Alter of the Holy Temple and looking into each other's eyes. From my seat on the witness chair, I watched as you held hands across that alter. I listened with tear filled eyes as the sealer joined you, my mother and my father, together for time and eternity. How can I ever repay our Heavenly Father for the privilege of kneeling at that same alter next to my parents and being sealed to them forever? How can I thank Him for sparing your life and granting our family the eternities? With God all things truly are possible.

Love,

Mike

When Barbara and I finished reading Mike's letter to a prodigal old Blackfeet Indian, I slowly folded it up and stuffed it back in the envelope. Then, taking her hand in mine, I drew her to me. We *were* going to spend the eternities together, with our sons, with their beautiful companions, and with *their* children. The road had been rough, and at times had seemed impossible. But we had stayed the course. We had stayed it until, with the truths of the Savior's gospel, we had at last found the way. We have been given a special spiritual gift. There is another gift, a wedding gift, that holds a special place in our hearts. Barbara gave me a music box that played a familiar tune--

"You were always on my mind."

Epilogue

Bob and Barbara Wren reside in Orem, Utah. They are employed by the Town of Eagle Mountain, Utah, where Barbara is the building department secretary, and Bob is the public utilities superintendent. They have eighteen grandchildren, five of whom have already served missions, and they have two great grandchildren. Barbara serves as Relief Society President and Bob is the High Priests Group Leader in their Orem ward. They will retire soon, but are already living happily ever after.

Bob and Barbara Wren, April 1956

Bob and Barbara Wren, April 2000

Do you know of an amazing and inspiring true story?

I am collecting such stories to be included in an upcoming book entitled, _O, My Father_. I am currently compiling stories, to be told from an LDS perspective, and will prepare the book with a dozen or so of these short stories. To be considered for publication, the stories must be true, spectacular, inspiring, uplifting, and so forth. The intent of telling these stories will be to promote the faith and hope of the reader, and to help each of us look to our Father in Heaven for His blessings, and to recognize His hand in our lives.

To submit a story, please write a very brief letter describing the event and it's highlights. If you are submitting a story about someone else, be sure to have their written permission before sending the information to me.

You may contact me, in writing, at the following address:

Michael S. Wren
975 East, 450 North
Heber City, UT 84032